Holt Spanish Level 1

¡Ven conmigo!®

Activities for Communication

HOLT, RINEHART AND WINSTON
Harcourt Brace & Company

Austin • New York • Orlando • Atlanta • San Francisco • Boston • Dallas • Toronto • London

Contributing Writers:

Rosann Batteiger

Mary Diehl

Richard Ezell

Felicia Kongable

Carol Ann Marshall

Amy Propps

Cover Photo/Illustration Credits
Group of students: Marty Granger/HRW Photo; tostada recipe: Annette Cable/Clare Jett & Assoc.

Art Credits
All art, unless otherwise noted, by Holt, Rinehart & Winston.
Page 1, Edson Campos; 2, Edson Campos; 3, Edson Campos; 4, Edson Campos; 11, Boston Graphics; 12, Boston Graphics; 17, Edson Campos; 18, Edson Campos; 21, Edson Campos; 22, Edson Campos; 27, Edson Campos; 28, Edson Campos; 39, Edson Campos; 40, Edson Campos; 63, Edson Campos; 64, Edson Campos.

Photo Credits
All photos by Marty Granger/Edge Video Productions/HRW except:
Page 75, Ragazza Magazine; 77, Reprinted by permission of Bayard Revistas from Súper Júnior, November 1996; 81, Mueblerias Berrios; 87, (all) Suplemento Fotogramas No. 1 Libro de Oro 50 Años de Cine from Fotogramas & Video, Año L, no. 1.843, 5/97 issue, p. 217–219, (br) "Braveheart" is a Twentieth Century Fox release, (cl) "Babe" is a Universal Studios release, (c) "Toy Story" is a Walt Disney production, distributed by Buena Vista; 101, (bl) Focus on Sports; (tr) Davis Madison/Duomo Photography; 120, (tl) A.T.&T. Photo Center/HRW; 120, (bl) Sam Dudgeon/HRW Photo; 130, M. L. Miller/Edge Video Productions/HRW.

¡VEN CONMIGO! is a registered trademark licensed to Holt, Rinehart and Winston.

Printed in the United States of America

ISBN 0-03-052604-3

1 2 3 4 5 6 7   021   03 02 01 00 99 98

Contents

SITUATION CARDS

To the Teacher

Oral communication is the most challenging language skill to develop and test. The *¡Ven conmigo! Activities for Communication* book helps students to develop their speaking skills and gives them opportunities to communicate in many different situations. The Communicative Activities and Situation Cards provide a variety of information-gap activities, role-plays, and interviews to assist students in modeling the progression from closed-ended practice to more creative, open-ended use of Spanish. The Realia reproduces authentic documents to provide students with additional reading practice using material written by and for native speakers. Included with the Realia are teaching suggestions and student activities showing how to integrate the four skills and culture into your realia lesson. With the focus on dialogue and real-life context, the activities in this book will help your students achieve the goal of genuine interaction.

Each chapter of *Activities for Communication* provides:

- **Communicative Activities** In each of the twelve chapters three communicative, pair-work activities encourage students to use Spanish in realistic conversation, in settings where they must seek and share information. The activities provide cooperative language practice and encourage students to take risks with language in a relaxed, uninhibiting, and enjoyable setting. The activities correspond to each **Paso** and encourage use of functions, vocabulary, and grammar presented in that chapter section. Each activity may be used upon completion of the **Paso** as a Performance Assessment, or may be recorded on audio or video tape for inclusion in students' portfolios. The activities may also be used as an informal review of the **Paso** to provide additional oral practice.

- **Realia** In each chapter there are three reproducible pieces of realia that relate to the chapter theme and reflect life and culture in Spanish-speaking countries. Finding they can read and understand documents intended for native speakers gives students a feeling of accomplishment that encourages them to continue learning. Upon completion of each **Paso**, the realia may be used to review the functions, vocabulary, and grammar presented, or may be used as additional practice at any point within the **Paso**. Along with the copying masters of the realia you will find suggestions for using the realia in the classroom. These suggestions include a combination of activities for individual, pair, and group work and focus on the skills of listening, speaking, reading, writing, and explore authentic cultural information.

- **Situation cards** Each of the twelve chapters contains three interviews and three situations for role-playing, one per **Paso**, in blackline master form. These cards are designed to stimulate conversation and to prepare students for speaking tests. The interviews or role-playing may be used as pair work with the entire class, as activities to begin the class period, as oral performance assessments upon completion of the **Paso**, or to encourage oral practice at any point during study of the **Paso**. These conversations may be recorded as audio or video additions to students' portfolios. Because the cards may be recycled throughout the scholastic year as review of chapters already completed, students will be rewarded as they realize they are meeting goals and improving their communicative abilities. To avoid having to copy the cards repeatedly, consider mounting them on cardboard and laminating them. They may be filed for use during the year, as well as for future classes.

Communicative
Activities

Communicative Activity 1-1A

1. **Situation** While you're at the mall on Saturday, you run into the new foreign exchange students from your school. Although you haven't met them yet, you recognize them from their school photos.

Task Use the clocks to determine the time of day and greet each of these people appropriately. Ask his or her name, and then ask each person how it's going or how he or she is. Write the information your partner gives you.

MODELO   A — **Buenos días. ¿Cómo te llamas?**
            B — **Me llamo...**
            A — **Mucho gusto. ¿Cómo estás?**
            B — **Estoy...**

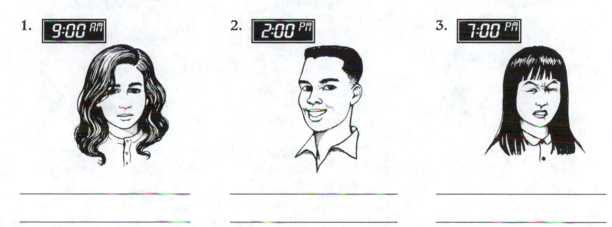

1. 9:00 AM
2. 2:00 PM
3. 7:00 PM

_____   _____   _____

_____   _____   _____

2. Now, pretend to be each of these students and answer your partner's questions.

MODELO   B — **Buenos días. ¿Cómo te llamas?**
            A — **Me llamo...**
            B — **Mucho gusto. ¿Cómo estás?**
            A — **Estoy...**

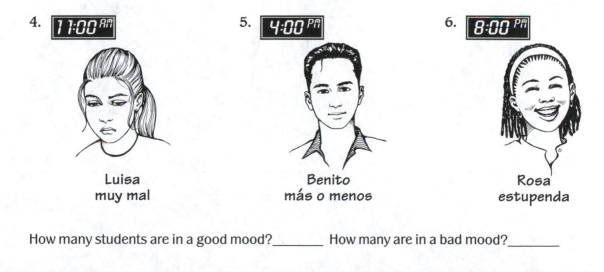

4. 11:00 AM
5. 4:00 PM
6. 8:00 PM

Luisa   Benito   Rosa
muy mal   más o menos   estupenda

How many students are in a good mood?_____ How many are in a bad mood?_____

COMMUNICATIVE ACTIVITIES

Communicative Activity 1-1 B

1. **Situation** While you're at the mall on Saturday, you run into the new foreign exchange students from your school. Although you haven't met them yet, you recognize them from their school photos.

Task Answer your partner's questions, pretending to be each of these students.

MODELO   A — **Buenos días. ¿Cómo te llamas?**
             B — **Me llamo...**
             A — **Mucho gusto. ¿Cómo estás?**
             B — **Estoy...**

1. **9:00 AM**

Adela
regular

2. **2:00 PM**

Diego
excelente

3. **7:00 PM**

Cristina
¡horrible!

2. Now switch roles. Use the clocks to determine the time of day and greet each of these students appropriately. Then ask each one's name, how it's going, or how she or he is. Write the information your partner gives you.

MODELO   B — **Buenos días. ¿Cómo te llamas?**
             A — **Me llamo...**
             B — **Mucho gusto. ¿Cómo estás?**
             A — **Estoy...**

4. **11:00 AM**

5. **4:00 PM**

6. **8:00 PM**

_____   _____   _____

_____   _____   _____

How many students are in a good mood? _____ How many are in a bad mood? _____

Communicative Activity 1-2A

Situation   You're helping your partner sort through the descriptions of pen pals for your Spanish Club. The photos got mislabeled.

Task   Match the descriptions to the photos. Ask your partner for the information you need for numbers two, three, and four. Then answer your partner's questions for numbers five, six, and seven.

MODELO   — El número 1, ¿cómo se llama?
— Se llama Juan Antonio Botero.
— ¿Cuántos años tiene?
— Tiene 16 años.
— ¿Y de dónde es?
— Es de Colombia.

1.

Juan Antonio Botero
16 años
Colombia

2.

_____

_____

_____

3.

_____

_____

_____

4.

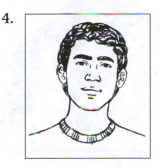

_____

_____

_____

5.

Pedro Serrano Marín
15 años
España

6.

Pilar Ríos Cabrillo
16 años
Colombia

7.

María Ángeles Castro Barrios
16 años
España

How many of the pen pals are 16 years old? _____ How many are from Spain? _____

Communicative Activity 1-2B

Situation You're helping your partner sort through the descriptions of pen pals for your Spanish Club. The photos got mislabeled.

Task Match the descriptions to the photos. Answer your partner's questions for numbers two, three, and four. Then ask your partner for the information you need for numbers five, six, and seven.

MODELO — El número 1, ¿cómo se llama?
— Se llama Juan Antonio Botero.
— ¿Cuántos años tiene?
— Tiene 16 años.
— ¿Y de dónde es?
— Es de Colombia.

1.
Juan Antonio Botero
16 años
Colombia

2.
María Elena Sánchez Orozco
14 años
México

3.
Juan Luis Portillo Benítez
16 años
Guatemala

4.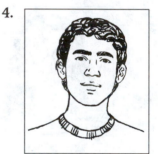
Lorenzo Malo Hernández
17 años
Ecuador

5.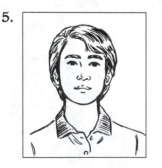

_____

_____

_____

6.

_____

_____

_____

7.

_____

_____

_____

How many of the pen pals are 16 years old? _____ How many are from Spain? _____

1. Situation You and your partner have won a trip to a beach resort for yourselves and your families. The only condition for your prize is that you must both decide on recreation, food, and music. Use the charts below to help you decide.

Task In the second chart, use the **Sí** column for your likes and the **No** column for your dislikes. Be sure to have two items for each category. Then answer your partner's questions about what you wrote.

MODELO   A — ¿Qué deporte te gusta?
            B — Me gusta el baloncesto.
            A — ¿Y también te gusta el voleibol?
            B — No, no me gusta el voleibol.

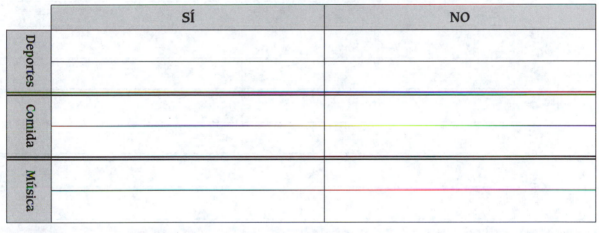

TU COMPAÑERO/A

	SÍ	NO
Deportes		
Comida		
Música		

TÚ

	SÍ	NO
Deportes		
Comida		
Música		

2. Now look at your two completed charts. Do you and your partner have some likes and dislikes in common? What are the two of you going to do, eat, and listen to during your beach vacation?

Communicative Activity 1-3B

1. Situation You and your partner have won a trip to a beach resort for yourselves and your families. The only condition for your prize is that you must both decide on recreation, food, and music. Use the charts below to help you decide.

Task In the second chart, use the **Sí** column for your likes and the **No** column for your dislikes. Be sure to have two items for each category. Then ask each other about what you wrote and write your partner's answers in the first chart.

MODELO   A — ¿Qué deporte te gusta?
         B — Me gusta el baloncesto.
         A — ¿Y también te gusta el voleibol?
         B — No, no me gusta el voleibol.

TU COMPAÑERO/A

	SÍ	NO
Deportes		
Comida		
Música		

TÚ

	SÍ	NO
Deportes		
Comida		
Música		

2. Now look at your two completed charts. Do you and your partner have some likes and dislikes in common? What are the two of you going to do, eat, and listen to during your beach vacation?

Communicative Activity 2-1A

1. **Situation** You're a clerk in a bookstore and your partner is a customer.

Task Find out what the customer wants and write his or her order on the receipt below. The bookstore is overstocked on backpacks and erasers, so if your customer doesn't ask for these items, be sure to ask if he or she needs them.

MODELO
A — Buenos días.
B — Necesito una mochila y siete cuadernos.
A — Muy bien. ¿También necesita unas gomas de borrar?
B — No, ya tengo gomas de borrar.
A — ¿Algo más?
B — Sí, necesito...

Librería Norte
RECIBO

2. Now switch roles. This time you're the customer and your partner is the clerk. Use your shopping list to tell the store clerk what you need.

MODELO
B — Buenas tardes.
A — Necesito una mochila y 2 carpetas.
B — Muy bien. ¿También necesita unos lápices?
A — No, ya tengo lápices.
B — ¿Algo más?
A — Sí, necesito...

Ya tengo...
1 cuaderno
muchas gomas de borrar
1 calculadora
1 regla
8 lápices

Necesito...
4 cuadernos más
3 bolígrafos
2 carpetas
1 mochila
1 diccionario

Who bought more items, you or your partner? _____

HRW material copyrighted under notice appearing earlier in this work.

COMMUNICATIVE ACTIVITIES

Communicative Activity 2-1B

1. **Situation** You're a customer in a bookstore and your partner is a clerk.

Task Use your shopping list to tell the store clerk what you need.

MODELO
A — Buenos días.
B — Necesito una mochila y siete cuadernos.
A — Muy bien. ¿También necesita unas gomas de borrar?
B — No, ya tengo gomas de borrar.
A — ¿Algo más?
B — Sí, necesito...

Ya tengo...	Necesito...
1 bolígrafo	1 carpeta
1 diccionario	11 lápices
2 gomas de borrar	7 cuadernos
	3 bolígrafos más
	1 mochila
	papel

2. Now switch roles. This time you're the clerk and your partner is a customer. The bookstore is over-stocked on calculators and pencils, so if your customer doesn't ask for these items, be sure to ask if he or she needs them.

MODELO
B — Buenas tardes.
A — Necesito una mochila y 2 carpetas.
B — Muy bien. ¿También necesita unos lápices?
A — No, ya tengo lápices.
B — ¿Algo más?
A — Sí, necesito...

Librería Norte
R E C I B O

Who bought more items, you or your partner? _____

Communicative Activity 2-2A

1. Situation You and your partner are working at a moving business during the summer. You're supposed to deliver the Rodríguez family's furniture, but you accidentally got the information for the Morales family.

Task Before you arrive at the Rodríguez's home, find out from your partner what belongs in each person's room.

MODELO   A — ¿Qué necesito poner en el cuarto de Marcos?
              B — En el cuarto de Marcos necesitas poner...

CLIENTE: *Familia Rodríguez*	
NOMBRE	**PERTENENCIAS**
Marcos	
José	
Carmen	

2. Now answer your partner's questions about the Morales home.

MODELO   B — ¿Qué necesito poner en el cuarto de Luisa?
              A — En el cuarto de Luisa necesitas poner...

CLIENTE: *Familia Morales*	
NOMBRE	**PERTENENCIAS**
Luisa	*2 camas, 1 silla, 1 escritorio, 2 lámparas, 1 radio, muchos carteles*
Juan	*1 cama, 1 escritorio, 1 lámpara, 1 televisor, 2 sillas, 1 reloj*
Marta	*1 cama, 1 silla, 2 mesas*

Who had to move more furniture, you or your partner? _____

COMMUNICATIVE ACTIVITIES

Communicative Activity 2-2B

1. Situation You and your partner are working at a moving business during the summer. You're supposed to deliver the Morales family's furniture, but you accidentally got the information for the Rodríguez family.

Task Answer your partner's questions about the Rodríguez's home.

MODELO   A — ¿Qué necesito poner en el cuarto de Marcos?
B — En el cuarto de Marcos necesitas poner...

CLIENTE: *Familia Rodríguez*	
NOMBRE	**PERTENENCIAS**
Marcos	*1 cama, 3 sillas, 1 mesa, unos carteles, 1 radio*
José	*2 camas, 1 silla, unos carteles, 3 mesas, 1 lámpara*
Carmen	*1 cama, 2 sillas, 1 televisor, 1 escritorio, 3 lámparas, 1 reloj*

2. Before you arrive at the Morales's home, find out from your partner what belongs in each person's room.

MODELO   B — ¿Qué necesito poner en el cuarto de Luisa?
A — En el cuarto de Luisa necesitas poner...

CLIENTE: *Familia Morales*	
NOMBRE	**PERTENENCIAS**
Luisa	
Juan	
Marta	

Who had to move more furniture, you or your partner? _____

Communicative Activity 2-3A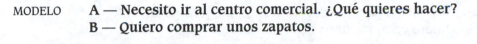

1. Situation You have a list of things you need to do this weekend and your partner has a list of things he or she wants to do.

Task Find out if there are things you might be able to do together by telling your partner what you're doing or where you're going. Then ask what he or she wants or needs to do. Write that down next to your list.

MODELO   A — Necesito ir al centro comercial. ¿Qué quieres hacer?

                   B — Quiero comprar unos zapatos.

el sábado

Necesito...

1. ir al centro comercial
2. organizar mi cuarto
3. hacer la tarea
4. comprar un diccionario de español

2. Now compare your lists. What will you be able to do together? What won't you be able to do together?

Communicative Activity 2-3B

1. **Situation** Your partner has a list of things he or she needs to do this weekend and you have a list of things you want to do.

   Task Find out if there are things you might be able to do together by answering your partner's questions and listening to what he or she says. Write down your partner's errands next to your list.

   MODELO   A — Necesito ir al centro comercial. ¿Qué quieres hacer?
   B — Quiero comprar unos zapatos.

   el sábado

   Quiero. . .

   1. comprar unos zapatos
   2. conocer a unos nuevos amigos
   3. encontrar mi dinero
   4. ir al la librería

2. Now compare your lists. What will you be able to do together? What won't you be able to do together?

Nombre _____ Clase _____ Fecha _____

1. Situation Classes start tomorrow morning. You and your partner accidentally received each other's class schedules for the new semester.

Task Ask your partner for the correct schedule information.

MODELO   A — ¿Qué clase tengo a las ocho y media?
B — La clase de ciencias.
A — ¿Cómo se llama el profesor?
B — Se llama el profesor Macías.

Hora	Clase	Profesor(a)
8:30-9:30	ciencias	el profesor Macías
9:30-10:30		
10:30-10:45	descanso	
10:45-11:45		
11:45-12:15	almuerzo	
12:15-1:15		
1:15-1:30	descanso	
1:30-2:30		
2:30-3:30		

2. Now give your partner the information to fill in her or his schedule.

MODELO   B — ¿Qué clase tengo a las ocho y media?
A — La clase de francés.
B — ¿Cómo se llama la profesora?
A — Se llama la profesora Bermondy.

Hora	Clase	Profesor(a)
8:30-9:30	francés	la profesora Bermondy
9:30-10:30	química	el profesor Peña
10:30-10:45	descanso	
10:45-11:45	coro	el profesor Méndez
11:45-12:15	almuerzo	
12:15-1:15	computación	la profesora Soto
1:15-1:30	descanso	
1:30-2:30	español	el profesor Galindo
2:30-3:30	geografía	la profesora Smith

What times during the day do your schedules match? _____ _____ _____ _____

HRW material copyrighted under notice appearing earlier in this work.

COMMUNICATIVE ACTIVITIES

Communicative Activity 3-1 B

1. Situation Classes start tomorrow morning. You and your partner accidentally received each other's class schedules for the new semester.

Task Give your partner the correct schedule information.

MODELO   A — ¿Qué clase tengo a las ocho y media?
              B — La clase de ciencias.
              A — ¿Cómo se llama el profesor?
              B — Se llama el profesor Macías.

Hora	Clase	Profesor(a)
8:30-9:30	ciencias	el profesor Macías
9:30-10:30	arte	la profesora Rodríguez
10:30-10:45	descanso	
10:45-11:45	inglés	el profesor García
11:45-12:15	almuerzo	
12:15-1:15	matemáticas	la profesora Díaz
1:15-1:30	descanso	
1:30-2:30	español	el profesor Galindo
2:30-3:30	ciencias sociales	el profesor Pérez

2. Now ask your partner for the information to fill in your schedule.

MODELO   B — ¿Qué clase tengo a las ocho y media?
              A — La clase de francés.
              B — ¿Cómo se llama la profesora?
              A — Se llama la profesora Bermondy.

Hora	Clase	Profesor(a)
8:30-9:30	francés	la profesora Bermondy
9:30-10:30		
10:30-10:45	descanso	
10:45-11:45		
11:45-12:15	almuerzo	
12:15-1:15		
1:15-1:30	descanso	
1:30-2:30		
2:30-3:30		

What times during the day do your schedules match? _____ _____ _____ _____

Nombre _____ Clase _____ Fecha _____

1. Situation You are staying in Cuernavaca for a week with your family. You call your partner who lives in town to find out about some of the events that are going on.

Task Your partner has a local entertainment guide and you have a newspaper. Some of the events listed are the same, but your newspaper has some missing information. Look at the schedule below and ask your partner for the information you need.

MODELO   A — ¿A qué hora es la clase de computacíon?
               B — A las seis y media.

2. Now answer your partner's questions about the following ads.

Write down two events that you'd both like to attend. _____

Communicative Activity 3-2B

1. Situation You live in Cuernavaca. Your partner is visiting from the United States and wants to find out about things to do in town for the week.

Task Your partner has a newspaper and you have a local entertainment guide. Some of the events listed are the same, but your entertainment guide has more complete information. Look at the schedule below and answer your partner's questions.

MODELO   A — ¿A qué hora es la clase de computacíon?
                B — A las seis y media.

2. Now switch roles and ask your partner about the following ads.

Write down two events that you'd both like to attend. _____

Communicative Activity 3-3A

1. Situation You and your partner are arranging photos of the new teachers for the yearbook.

Task Answer your partner's questions to match his or her photos with the correct name.

MODELO   B — ¿Cómo es la Sra. Alvarado?
          A — Es alta, rubia, e inteligente.

NOMBRE	¿CÓMO ES?
Sra. Alvarado	alta, rubia, inteligente
Sr. Dávila	alto, moreno, guapo, estricto
Sr. Carrillo	bajo, rubio, cómico
Srta. Camacho	alta, morena, simpática
Sra. Franco	alta, morena, bonita, estricta
Sr. González	bajo, moreno, simpático, cómico

2. Now ask your partner what each teacher on your list is like. Match the names to the photos according to your partner's description. You have photos of Sr. Gutiérrez, Srta. Guzmán, Sra. Benavides, Sr. Romero, Sra. Fernández, and Sr. García.

MODELO   A — ¿Cómo es el Sr. García?
          B — Es alto, moreno, estricto y antipático.

Sr. García

_____   _____   _____

_____   _____   _____

Which teachers' classes would you most enjoy? _____ and _____

Why? _____

Communicative Activity 3-3B

1. **Situation** You and your partner are arranging photos of the new teachers for the yearbook.

Task Ask your partner what each teacher on your list is like. Match the names to the photos according to your partner's description. You have photos of Sra. Alvaredo, Sr. Dávila, Srta. Camacho, Sr. Carrillo, Sra. Franco, and Sr. González.

MODELO   B — ¿Cómo es la Sra. Alvarado?
                A — Es alta, rubia, e inteligente.

_____ _____ _____

_____ _____ Sra. Alvarado

2. Now answer your partner's questions to match her or his photos with the correct name.

MODELO   A — ¿Cómo es el Sr. García?
                B — Es alto, moreno, estricto y antipático

NOMBRE	¿CÓMO ES?
Sr. Gutiérrez	alto, rubio, guapo, simpático
Srta. Guzmán	alta, bonita, morena, cómica
Sra. Benavides	rubia, simpática, interesante
Sr. Romero	bajo, moreno, guapo, aburrido
Sra. Fernández	baja, rubia, inteligente
Sr. García	alto, moreno, estricto, antipático

Which teachers' classes would you most enjoy? _____ and _____

Why? _____

Communicative Activity 4-1 A

1. Situation You and your partner are working on the school newspaper. You've been assigned to interview a number of new exchange students, so you've divided the interviews.

Task Ask your partner questions about his or her interviews to complete the article for the paper.

MODELO   A — ¿Qué le gusta hacer a Julio?
           B — A Julio le gusta montar en bicicleta. También le gusta...

Julio	Martín	José Luis
montar en bicicleta		

2. Now help your partner by sharing the information you have from your interviews.

MODELO   B — ¿Qué le gusta hacer a Amelia?
           A — A Amelia le gusta ir a fiestas. También le gusta...

Amelia	Guadalupe	Lorena
ir a fiestas	escuchar música	practicar deportes
pasar el rato con amigos	pintar	hablar con amigos
caminar en el parque	nadar	escuchar música
escuchar música	tocar el piano	montar en bicicleta

How many of the students enjoy sports? _____ swimming? _____ painting? _____

Communicative Activity 4-1 B

1. Situation You and your partner are working on the school newspaper. You've been assigned to interview a number of new exchange students, so you've divided the interviews.

Task Answer your partner's questions about your interviews to complete the article for the paper.

MODELO 　　A — ¿Qué le gusta hacer a Julio?
　　　　　　B — A Julio le gusta montar en bicicleta. También le gusta...

Julio	Martín	José Luis
montar en bicicleta	tocar la guitarra	ir a fiestas
pasar el rato con amigos	pintar	escuchar música
practicar deportes	practicar deportes	caminar en el parque
nadar	escuchar música	pasar el rato con amigos

2. Now ask your partner questions to get the information he or she has from the interviews.

MODELO 　　B — ¿Qué le gusta hacer a Amelia?
　　　　　　A — A Amelia le gusta ir a fiestas. También le gusta...

Amelia	Guadalupe	Lorena
ir a fiestas		

How many of the students enjoy sports? _____ swimming? _____ painting? _____

Nombre _____ Clase _____ Fecha _____

1. Situation Your partner borrowed several of your things. He or she returned them to your room, but you can't find them because they're not where they belong.

Task Ask your partner where each of these items is. Based on your partner's answer, mark its location on the drawing of your room.

MODELO   A — ¿Dónde está mi libro de francés?
B — Está cerca del estante.

diccionario	libro de francés	videojuego	radio

2. Now switch roles. Answer your partner's questions about where you returned her or his items according to this drawing.

Compare your answers to be sure you each marked the items as they appear in the drawings.

¡Ven conmigo! Level 1, Chapter 4   Activities for Communication **21**

HRW material copyrighted under notice appearing earlier in this work.

COMMUNICATIVE ACTIVITIES

Communicative Activity 4-2B

1. Situation You borrowed several of your partner's things. You returned them to your partner's room, but he or she can't find them because they're not where they belong.

Task Answer your partner's questions about each item's location according to the drawing.

MODELO   A — ¿Dónde está mi libro de francés?
              B — Está cerca del estante.

2. Now switch roles. Ask your partner where she or he placed these items in your room. Mark each one on the drawing of your room.

mochila   calculadora   lápiz   libro de geografía

Compare your answers to be sure you each marked the items as they appear in the drawings.

Communicative Activity 4-3A

1. Situation You and your partner are secret agents trying to crack a suspected spy ring. You have followed a man with the codename "**Liebre**". Your partner has followed a woman codenamed "**Ardilla**".

Task Ask your partner for the information he or she has obtained on "**Ardilla**". If there is a day that your partner doesn't have information for, put an X in the blank.

MODELO   A — ¿Adónde va "Ardilla" los martes?
                    B — Los martes a las seis de la tarde va al supermercado.

Las actividades de "Ardilla"		
día	**hora**	**¿adónde va?**
los lunes		
los martes	6:00 p.m.	al supermercado
los miércoles		
los jueves		
los viernes		
los sábados		
los domingos		

2. Now answer your partner's questions about "**Liebre**" according to these photos. If there is a day where you don't have a photo, tell your partner, "**No sé.**"

MODELO   B — ¿Adónde va "Liebre" los lunes?
                    A — Los lunes a las ocho de la mañana va a la piscina.

los lunes, 8 a.m.   los domingos, 9 a.m.   los jueves, 7:30 p.m.

los sábados, 4 p.m.   los martes, 1 p.m.   los miércoles, 6 p.m.

Is there a time and place during the week that the two suspects might be meeting to exchange information? _____

Communicative Activity 4-3B

1. Situation You and your partner are secret agents trying to crack a suspected spy ring. You have followed a woman with the codename "**Ardilla**". Your partner has followed a man codenamed "**Liebre**".

Task Answer your partner's questions about "**Ardilla**" according to these photos. If there is a day where you don't have a photo, tell your partner, "**No sé.**"

MODELO   A — ¿Adónde va "Ardilla" los martes?
                  B — Los martes a las seis de la tarde va al supermercado.

los sábados, 4 p.m.

los miércoles, 7:30 p.m.

los viernes, 8 p.m.

los jueves, 2 p.m.

los domingos, 9:30 a.m.

los martes, 6 p.m.

2. Now ask your partner for the information he or she has obtained on "**Liebre**". If there is a day that your partner doesn't have information for, put an X in the blank.

MODELO   B — ¿Adónde va "Liebre" los lunes?
                  A — Los lunes a las ocho de la mañana va a la piscina.

Las actividades de "Liebre"		
día	hora	¿adónde va?
los lunes	8:00 a.m.	a la piscina
los martes		
los miércoles		
los jueves		
los viernes		
los sábados		
los domingos		

Is there a time and place during the week that the two suspects might be meeting to exchange information? _____

1. Situation You and your partner have just completed a survey for your PE class on the health habits of 100 students in your school.

Task Ask your partner for the information she or he has compiled from the survey. Fill in the chart with the numbers your partner gives you.

MODELO   A — ¿Cuántos estudiantes nunca asisten a una clase de ejercicios aeróbicos?
            B — Veintisiete estudiantes.
            A — ¿Y a veces?
            B — Cuarenta y tres estudiantes.
            A — ¿Y todos los días?
            B — Treinta estudiantes.

	nunca	a veces	todos los días
asistir a una clase de ejercicios aeróbicos	27	43	30
comer ensalada			
correr dos millas			
tomar refrescos			
practicar un deporte			

2. Now help your partner complete the chart by answering his or her questions. Use the information you've compiled below.

	nunca	a veces	todos los días
comer hamburguesas con papas fritas	10	64	26
desayunar	2	79	19
comer frutas	5	80	15
mirar mucha televisión	11	25	64
caminar	2	10	88

Compare both charts. Which activity do the most students participate in . . .

every day? _____

sometimes? _____

never? _____

Communicative Activity 5-1B

1. Situation You and your partner have just completed a survey for your PE class on the health habits of 100 students in your school.

Task Help your partner complete the chart by answering his or her questions. Use the information you've compiled below.

MODELO A — ¿Cuántos estudiantes nunca asisten a una clase de ejercicios aeróbicos?
B — Veintisiete estudiantes.
A — ¿Y a veces?
B — Cuarenta y tres estudiantes.
A — ¿Y todos los días?
B — Treinta estudiantes.

	nunca	a veces	todos los días
asistir a una clase de ejercicios aeróbicos	27	43	30
comer ensalada	18	71	11
correr dos millas	63	28	9
tomar resfrescos	14	49	37
practicar un deporte	19	47	34

2. Now switch roles. Ask your partner for the information she or he has compiled from the survey. Fill in the chart with the numbers your partner gives you.

	nunca	a veces	todos los días
comer hamburguesas con papas fritas			
desayunar			
comer frutas			
mirar mucha televisión			
caminar			

Compare both charts. Which activity do the most students participate in . . .

every day? _____

sometimes? _____

never? _____

Communicative Activity 5-2A

1. Situation You and your partner both have friends visiting you in Miami over the holiday break. You want to invite both groups of friends to do various activities.

Task Ask your partner which activities his or her guests like. Mark each one in the chart below.

MODELO   A — ¿Qué le gusta a Roberto?
B — Le gusta nadar.
A — ¿Le gusta nadar a Lola?
B — No, no le gusta nadar pero le gusta leer novelas.

	nadar	bucear	leer novelas	esquiar	jugar a un deporte	pescar
Roberto	X					
Lola			X			
Graciela						
Melisa						
Alejandro						
Luis						

2. Now answer your partner's questions about the other guests according to the pictures below.

MODELO   B — ¿Qué le gusta a Mariana?
A — Le gusta correr.
B — ¿Le gusta correr a Gregorio?
A — No, no le gusta correr pero le gusta asistir a bailes.

Mariana   Gregorio   Isabel

Carlos   Raquel   Esteban

How many of all the guests seem to prefer active pastimes? _____

Communicative Activity 5-2B

1. Situation You and your partner both have friends visiting you in Miami over the holiday break. You want to invite both groups of friends to do various activities.

Task Answer your partner's questions about which activities your guests like to do according to the drawings below.

MODELO   A — ¿Qué le gusta a Roberto?
               B — Le gusta nadar.
               A — ¿Le gusta nadar a Lola?
               B — No, no le gusta nadar pero le gusta leer novelas.

     Roberto   Lola   Graciela

     Melisa   Alejandro   Luis

2. Now ask your partner about her or his guests' favorite activities. Mark the information in the chart below.

MODELO   B — ¿Qué le gusta a Mariana?
               A — Le gusta correr.
               B — ¿Le gusta correr a Gregorio?
               A — No, no le gusta correr pero le gusta asistir a bailes.

	acampar	hacer ejercicio	correr	descansar	escribir tarjetas postales	asistir a bailes
Mariana			X			
Gregorio						X
Isabel						
Carlos						
Raquel						
Esteban						

How many of all the guests seem to prefer active pastimes? _____

Nombre _____ Clase _____ Fecha _____

Communicative Activity 5-3A

1. **Situation** You and your partner are writing a travel column for your local newspaper. Your readers will want to know about the weather in different areas of the U.S.

Task Ask your partner about the weather in each of the following cities. Fill in the chart with the information he or she gives you.

MODELO   A — ¿Qué tiempo hace en Omaha en enero?
          B — Está nublado y nieva mucho.

Ciudad	enero	julio
Omaha	está nublado, nieva mucho	
St. Louis		
Dallas		
Denver		
Indianapolis		

2. Now answer your partner's questions about the weather in each of the following cities. Use the information you have in the chart below.

MODELO   B — ¿Qué tiempo hace en Olympia en julio?
          A — Hace sol y hace viento.

Ciudad	enero	julio
Olympia		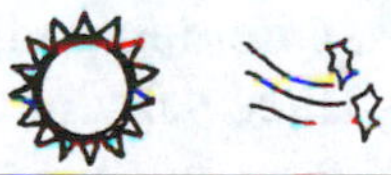
Seattle		
Portland		
Boise		
San Francisco	 30° F	

In which cities would you need to carry an umbrella in the winter? _____

Which cities have the most similar weather in July? _____

Communicative Activity 5-3B

1. Situation You and your partner are writing a travel column for your local newspaper. Your readers will want to know about the weather in different areas of the U.S.

Task Answer your partner's questions about the weather in each of the following cities. Use the information you have in the chart below.

MODELO   A — ¿Qué tiempo hace en Omaha en enero?
                B — Está nublado y nieva mucho.

Ciudad	enero	julio
Omaha		
St. Louis		
Dallas		
Denver		
Indianapolis		

2. Now ask your partner about the weather in each of the following cities. Fill in the chart with the information she or he gives you.

MODELO   B — ¿Qué tiempo hace en Olympia en julio?
                A — Hace sol y hace viento.

Ciudad	enero	julio
Olympia		hace sol y hace viento
Seattle		
Portland		
Boise		
San Francisco		

In which cities would you need to carry an umbrella in the winter? _____

Which cities have the most similar weather in July? _____

1. Situation You and your partner are distant cousins collecting information for your entire family tree. You each have all the information about one family, but only some of the information about the other.

Task Ask your partner questions that will help you fill in the missing family names for the Santos family.

MODELO   A — ¿Quién es la hermana de Elena?
                B — La hermana de Elena es Julia.

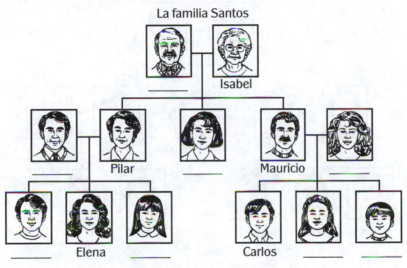

2. Now answer your partner's questions about the Reyes family.

MODELO   B — ¿Quién es el esposo de Rosa?
                A — El esposo de Rosa es Julio.

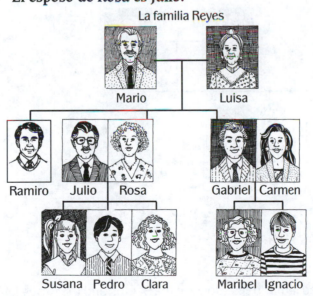

Compare your completed family trees. How are the Santos and the Reyes families related?

_____

COMMUNICATIVE ACTIVITIES

Communicative Activity 6-1 B

1. Situation You and your partner are distant cousins collecting information for your entire family tree. You each have all the information about one family, but only some of the information about the other.

Task Answer your partner's questions about the Santos family.

MODELO   A — ¿Quién es la hermana de Elena?
               B — La hermana de Elena es Julia.

La familia Santos

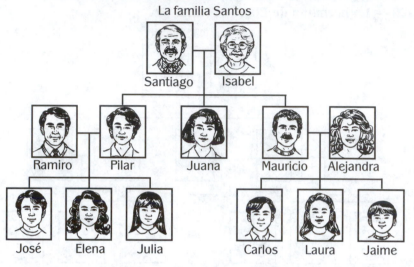

2. Now ask your partner for the missing names in the Reyes family.

MODELO   B — ¿Quién es el esposo de Rosa?
               A — El esposo de Rosa es Julio.

La familia Reyes

Compare your completed family trees. How are the Santos and the Reyes families related?

_____

Communicative Activity 6-2A

1. Situation You and your partner have just finished your first day in a new school, and you are comparing notes about your new classmates.

Task Your partner has only some of the information in the following chart. Without saying the student's name, read the list of characteristics for each student. Your partner will fill in the blanks on her or his chart and guess the student's name.

MODELO   A — Él tiene pelo negro, ojos negros, y no es ni alto ni bajo...
         B — ¿Es Rogelio?
         A — Sí, es Rogelio.

Rogelio	Encarnación	Manrique	Mercedes
pelo negro	rubia	pelo castaño	pelirroja
ojos negros	ojos de color café	ojos azules	ojos verdes
ni alto ni bajo	alta	alto	baja
delgado	no delgada	no delgado	delgada

2. Now, talk about what each person is like. You find that your partner has focused on their good qualities, while you saw only the negative ones. Tell your partner what you think of each person, and fill in the blanks with what he or she has to add.

MODELO   B — ¿Cómo es Juan Carlos?
         A — Bueno, es egoísta.
         B — Pero también es romántico y atlético.

	Juan Carlos	Silvia	Rosa	Victor
Calidades Buenas	_____ _____	_____ _____	_____ _____	_____ _____
Calidades Malas	egoísta	aburrida	perezosa	desorganizado

Which person do you think is most interesting? _____

Why? _____

_____

Communicative Activity 6-2B

1. **Situation** You and your partner have just finished your first day in a new school, and you are comparing notes about your new classmates. Your partner remembers more about each student than you do.

   Task Listen while your partner describes a student. Try to guess who your partner is talking about. Fill in the blanks before trying to guess.

   MODELO   A — Él tiene pelo negro, ojos negros, y no es ni alto ni bajo...

                   B — ¿Es Rogelio?

                   A — Sí, es Rogelio.

Rogelio	Encarnación	Manrique	Mercedes
pelo negro	_____	pelo castaño	_____
_____	_____	ojos azules	ojos verdes
ni alto ni bajo	alta	_____	baja
_____	no delgada	_____	_____

2. Now, talk about what each person is like. You find that your partner has focused on their negative qualities, while you saw the good ones. Fill in the blanks with what your partner says about each person; then try to set him or her straight!

   MODELO   B — ¿Cómo es Juan Carlos?

                   A — Bueno, es egoista.

                   B — ¡Pero también es romántico y atlético!

	Juan Carlos	Silvia	Rosa	Victor
Calidades Buenas	romántico, atlético	trabajadora, responsable	leal, generosa	artístico, creativo
Calidades Malas	_____	_____	_____	_____

Which person do you think is most interesting? _____

Why? _____

_____

Nombre ______________________ Clase ______________ Fecha ______________

Communicative Activity 6-3A

1. Situation You have asked your friends to help you with the chores so you can all attend a party together. Your partner has helped you organize the chores into an upstairs list **(arriba)** and a downstairs and outside list **(abajo y afuera)**.

Task Fill in the chart below by asking your partner what each of your friends should do upstairs.

MODELO **A — ¿Qué debe hacer Santiago?**
B — Santiago debe hacer la cama.

Arriba... ***(Upstairs)***

NOMBRE	**Santiago**	**Alicia**	**Oralia**	**Jaime**	**Eduardo**
QUEHACER					

2. Now answer your partner's questions about which downstairs and outside task **(abajo y afuera)** each friend should do.

Abajo y afuera... ***(Downstairs and outside)***

NOMBRE	**Orieta**	**Beatriz**	**Roberto**	**Rosana**	**Enrique**
QUEHACER	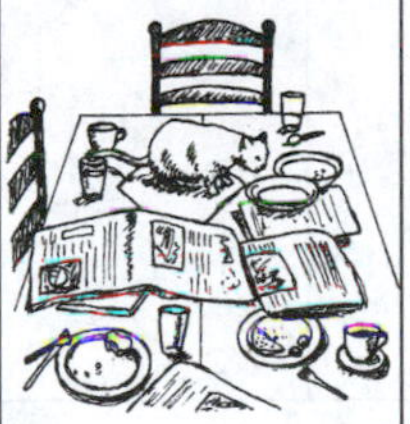	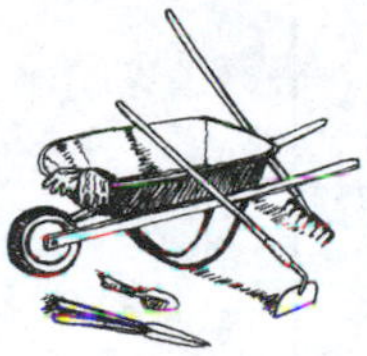	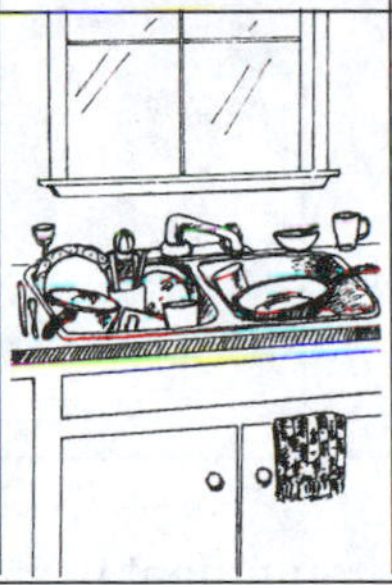	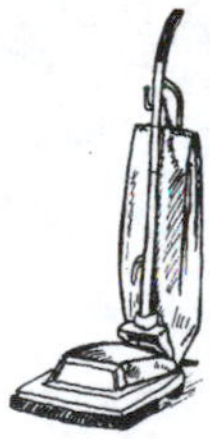	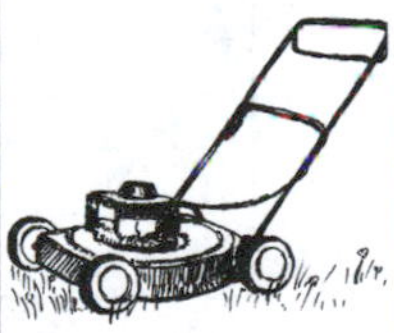

Which friends need to share equipment to finish their chores? ______________ and ______________

Communicative Activity 6-3B

1. Situation Your partner has asked his or her friends to help with the chores so you can all attend a party together. You've helped organize the chores into an upstairs list (**arriba**) and a downstairs and outside list (**abajo y afuera**).

Task Answer your partner's questions about which upstairs task each friend should do.

MODELO   A — ¿Qué debe hacer Santiago?
                  B — Santiago debe hacer la cama.

Arriba... *(Upstairs)*

NOMBRE	Santiago	Alicia	Oralia	Jaime	Eduardo
QUEHACER					

2. Now, to fill in the chart below, ask your partner which downstairs and outside task (**abajo y afuera**) each friend should do.

Abajo y afuera... *(Downstairs and outside)*

NOMBRE	Orieta	Beatriz	Roberto	Rosana	Enrique
QUEHACER					

Which friends need to share equipment to finish their chores? _____ and _____

Nombre _____ Clase _____ Fecha _____

1. Situation You're the switchboard operator at a hotel, in charge of taking messages for hotel guests. Your partner will call to talk to some people staying at the hotel.

Task First answer the phone, then check your chart to see whether the guest your partner asks for is available. If he or she is out, take a message and write it in the chart below.

MODELO   A — Diga.
                 B — ¿Está Anita Jáquez Franco?
                 A — No está en su habitación. ¿Quiere dejar un recado?
                 B — Soy el tío Mario. La boda empieza a las tres.

Huésped	Datos	Recado
Anita Jáquez Franco	no está en su habitación	Tío Mario: la boda empieza a las tres
Santiago Fuentes Alarcón	está en el restaurante	
Maricarmen Fernández	la línea está ocupada	
Federico Montes	regresa a las diez	
César Ramírez	sale a correr	

2. Now, call your partner and ask for each of the following guests. If your partner tells you they're not available, identify yourself and leave a message using the notes below.

MODELO   B — Diga.
                 A — ¿Está Ana María Sánchez?
                 B — Ya sale en taxi. ¿Quiere dejar un recado?
                 A — Soy Marcela López. Vamos al teatro mañana por la noche.

Ana María Sánchez	Marcela López: vamos al teatro mañana por la noche
Héctor Paredes	la tía Beatriz: la fiesta de graduación empieza a las diez
Pedro Enríquez Castro	Umberto Díaz: Vamos a desayunar mañana; invito yo
Margarita Cruz García	Juana Izurieta: ¿está lista para ir?; ya venimos
Alejandro Zaragosa	Mauricio Peña: ¿a qué hora quiere salir?

How many of the guests were out of their rooms when you called? _____

Communicative Activity 7-1 B

1. Situation You're trying to get in touch with some people who are staying at the hotel where your partner works as the switchboard operator.

Task Call the hotel and ask for each person. If the guest you're calling isn't available, identify yourself and leave the following messages.

MODELO   A — Diga.
B — ¿Está Anita Jáquez Franco?
A — No está en su habitación. ¿Quiere dejar un recado?
B — Soy el tío Mario. La boda empieza a las tres.

Anita Jáquez Franco	el tío Mario: la boda empieza a las tres
Federico Montes	su hermana: venimos a las diez y media
Santiago Fuentes Alarcón	Jessica: ¿quiere desayunar conmigo mañana?
Maricarmen Fernández	Yolanda Reyes: ¿por qué siempre está ocupada la línea?
César Ramírez	su papá: ¿puede llamar a casa?

2. Now, you're the operator taking messages for the hotel guests. Answer the phone, then check your chart to see whether the guest your partner asks for is available. If he or she is out, take a message.

MODELO   B — Diga.
A — ¿Está Ana María Sánchez?
B — Ya sale en taxi. ¿Quiere dejar un recado?
A — Soy Marcela López. Vamos al teatro mañana por la noche.

Huésped	Datos	Recado
Ana María Sánchez	ya sale en taxi	Marcela López: vamos al teatro mañana por la noche
Margarita Cruz García	regresa a las nueve	
Héctor Paredes	está en la piscina	
Pedro Enríquez Castro	no está	
Alejandro Zaragosa	asiste a una conferencia	

How many of the guests were out of their rooms when you called? _____

HRW material copyrighted under notice appearing earlier in this work.

Communicative Activity 7-2A

1. Situation Your best friend Jorge's birthday is this Friday. You want to celebrate by having a surprise party. You're calling the rest of your friends to make plans.

Task Call your friends on the list below and ask them what they're doing Friday. Tell them about the surprise party. Invite them over to your house.

MODELO
A — Hola, Diana, ¿qué piensas hacer el viernes?
B — El viernes voy a visitar a mi abuela.
A — ¿Por qué no vienes a mi casa? Es el cumpleaños de Jorge y le voy a hacer una fiesta de sorpresa.
B — Lo siento, pero quiero ver a mi abuela. or ¡Qué bueno! ¿A qué hora?

> Diana
> Pedro Arturo
> Ronaldo
> Susana
> Ana Carla
> Cristóbal y su hermana

2. Now, switch roles. Look at the drawings below. When your partner calls, tell her or him what you plan to do this Saturday. Decide whether you can change your plans and tell your partner.

MODELO
B — Hola, Ernesto, ¿qué piensas hacer el sábado?
A — El sábado pienso ir al lago con mi papá.
B — ¿Por qué no vienes a mi casa? Es el cumpleaños de Paco y le voy a hacer una fiesta de sorpresa.
A — Me gustaría, pero voy al lago. or ¡Cómo no! ¿A qué hora?

Ernesto

Marco

Linda

Samuel y su hermano

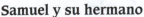
Blanca

Rebeca

How many friends turn down your invitation to go elsewhere? _____

How many will be coming to your party? _____

Activities for Communication **39**

COMMUNICATIVE ACTIVITIES

Communicative Activity 7-2B

1. Situation Your partner is calling about his or her best friend Jorge's birthday this Friday. He or she wants to celebrate by having a surprise party.

Task Look at the drawings below. When your partner calls, tell her or him what you plan to do this Saturday. Decide whether you can change your plans and tell your partner.

MODELO
A — Hola, Diana, ¿qué piensas hacer el viernes?
B — El viernes voy a visitar a mi abuela.
A — ¿Por qué no vienes a mi casa? Es el cumpleaños de Jorge y le voy a hacer una fiesta de sorpresa.
B — Lo siento, pero quiero ver a mi abuela. or ¡Qué bueno! ¿A qué hora?

Diana

Pedro Arturo

Ronaldo

Susana

Ana Carla

Cristobal y su hermana

2. Now, switch roles. Your best friend Paco is having a birthday and you're organizing a surprise party this Saturday. Call your friends on the list below, ask about their plans for Saturday, and invite them over to your house.

MODELO
B — Hola, Ernesto, ¿qué piensas hacer el sábado?
A — El sábado pienso ir al lago con mi papá.
B — ¿Por qué no vienes a mi casa? Es el cumpleaños de Paco y le voy a hacer una fiesta de sorpresa.
A — Me gustaría, pero voy al lago. or ¡Cómo no! ¿A qué hora?

> Ernesto
> Marco
> Linda
> Samuel y su hermano
> Blanca
> Rebeca

How many friends turn down your invitation to go elsewhere? _____

How many will be coming to your party? _____

Communicative Activity 7-3A

1. Situation You call to get together with your partner, but you both have very busy schedules.

Task Find a time this weekend when you're both free. Invite your partner to the events listed, and don't stop until he or she accepts your invitation.

MODELO
A — Te gustaría ir al campo el sábado por la tarde?
B — ¿El sábado? Lo siento, pero no puedo. Voy a estar todo el día con los abuelos.
A — ¡Qué lástima! Entonces, ¿quieres...?

> ir al campo el sábado por la tarde
> ir a una fiesta el jueves por la noche
> caminar en el parque el lunes por la tarde
> ir al teatro el viernes por la noche
> ir al acuario el miércoles después de clases

2. Now your partner calls to ask if you can get together this weekend. For each invitation, check your datebook to see if you're free. Accept the invitation if you can; if you're not free, turn it down and explain why.

MODELO
B — ¿Te gustaría ir al parque de atracciones el martes por la tarde?
A — ¿El martes? Lo siento, pero tengo tarea de química. Tengo que leer el capítulo 9.
B — ¡Qué lástima! Entonces, ¿quieres...?

DÍA Y FECHA	EVENTOS Y CITAS
domingo, 14 de marzo	necesito estudiar
lunes, 15 de marzo	mucha tarea: composición de inglés
martes, 16 de marzo	tarea de química: leer el capítulo 9
miércoles, 17 de marzo	partido de fútbol a las 6
jueves, 18 de marzo	ir al zoológico después de clases
viernes, 19 de marzo	mirar la televisión; ¡qué aburrido!
sábado, 20 de marzo	visitar a mi tío a las 4

Now, write what you and your partner have decided to do:

El _____ a las _____, vamos a _____.

Communicative Activity 7-3B

1. Situation Your partner calls you to see if you can get together this weekend.

Task For each invitation from your partner, check your datebook to see if you're free. Accept the invitation if you can; if you aren't free, turn it down and explain why.

MODELO A — Te gustaría ir al campo el sábado por la tarde?
        B — ¿El sábado? Lo siento, pero no puedo. Voy a estar todo el día con
            los abuelos.
        A — ¡Qué lástima! Entonces, ¿quieres...?

DÍA Y FECHA	EVENTOS Y CITAS
domingo, 14 de marzo	salir con la familia
lunes, 15 de marzo	biblioteca a las 7 con Marimar; geografía capítulo 8
martes, 16 de marzo	piscina con Jorge, a las 4; tarea de inglés
miércoles, 17 de marzo	¡qué día más aburrido!
jueves, 18 de marzo	estudiar para el examen de matemáticas
viernes, 19 de marzo	examen de matemáticas; fiesta de José Luis, a las 9
sábado, 20 de marzo	todo el día con los abuelos

2. You want to get together with your partner, but you both have very busy schedules. Find a time this weekend when you're both free. Invite your partner to the events listed, and don't stop until he or she accepts your invitation.

MODELO B — ¿Te gustaría ir al parque de atracciones el martes por la tarde?
        A — ¿El martes? Lo siento, pero tengo tarea de química. Tengo que leer
            el capítulo 9.
        B — ¡Qué lástima! Entonces, ¿quieres...?

> ir al parque de atracciones el martes por la tarde
> ir a comer a un restaurante el miércoles a las seis
> ir al cine el lunes por la tarde
> ir a una fiesta de cumpleaños el viernes a las nueve
> ir al lago a nadar el domingo por la tarde

Now, write what you and your partner have decided to do:

El _____ a las _____, vamos a _____.

Communicative Activity 8-1 A

1. Situation You and your partner are planning a lunch for a group of friends. Both of you've been asking around to find out what everyone likes and doesn't like so you'll know what to serve. You've spoken to José and Laura, and your partner has spoken to Claudia and Martín.

Task Find out from your partner what Claudia and Martín like and don't like. Complete the chart below with your partner's answers.

MODELO **A — ¿Qué le gusta a Claudia?**
B — Pues, a Claudia le gusta el atún.

	Le encanta(n)	Le gusta(n)	No le gusta(n) para nada
José	la sopa de pollo las manzanas	los refrescos	las toronjas
Claudia			
Laura	el queso	los perros calientes	el atún
Martín			

2. Now, you and your partner need to plan the menu for lunch. Use the information in the completed chart to list what you're going to serve.

Pensamos servir	No vamos a servir

Communicative Activity 8-1 B

1. Situation You and your partner are planning a lunch for a group of friends. Both of you've been asking around to find out what everyone likes and doesn't like so you'll know what to serve. You've spoken to Claudia and Martín, and your partner has spoken to José and Laura.

Task Find out from your partner what José and Laura like and don't like. Complete the chart below with your partner's answers.

MODELO   B — ¿Qué no le gusta a José?
A — Pues, a José no le gustan las toronjas.

	Le encanta(n)	Le gusta(n)	No le gusta(n) para nada
José			
Claudia	el atún	el arroz	las papitas los plátanos
Laura			
Martín	la crema de maní	los sandwiches de jamón	las legumbres

2. Now, you and your partner need to plan the menu for lunch. Use the information in the completed chart to list what you're going to serve.

Pensamos servir	No vamos a servir

¡Ven conmigo! Level 1, Chapter 8

Communicative Activity 8-2A

1. Situation You and your partner are reporting on a restaurant called "Chulita's" for your school paper. You are at the restaurant together, having a meal.

Task Ask about what your partner is having, and fill in the blanks in the chart.

MODELO **A — ¿Cómo está el pollo?**
B — Está muy salado.

Your partner's meal:

Comida	Comentario *(Comments)*
el pollo	muy salado
las legumbres	
la sopa	
el arroz	
la leche	
el flan	

2. Now, talk about the food you ordered. Answer your partner's questions with information from the following chart.

MODELO **B — ¿Te gusta el perro caliente?**
A — Sí, está muy rico.

Your meal:

Comida	Comentario *(Comments)*
el perro caliente	muy rico
los frijoles	calientes y deliciosos
el pan tostado	frío y horrible
el café con leche	demasiado dulce
la papaya	exquisita
las galletas	deliciosas

Which food will you recommend, and why? ____

Which one of you enjoyed your meal the most? ____

Communicative Activity 8-2B

1. Situation You and your partner are reporting on a restaurant called "Chulita's" for your school paper. You are at the restaurant together, having a meal.

Task Answer your partner's questions about the food you ordered.

MODELO   A — ¿Cómo está el pollo?
               B — Está muy salado.

Your meal:

Comida	Comentario *(Comments)*
el pollo	muy salado
las legumbres	frías pero ricas
la sopa	demasiado picante
el arroz	delicioso
la leche	fría y muy buena
el flan	muy rico

2. Now, ask about what your partner is having, and fill in the blanks in the chart.

MODELO   B — ¿Te gusta el perro caliente?
               A — Sí, está muy rico.

Your partner's meal:

Comida	Comentario *(Comments)*
el perro caliente	muy rico
los frijoles	
el pan tostado	
el café con leche	
la papaya	
las galletas	

Which food will you recommend, and why? _____

Which one of you enjoyed your meal the most? _____

Communicative Activity 8-3A

1. Situation You're a waiter working at a restaurant. Your partner is a customer who would like to order from the daily specials menu, but the items are listed without their prices.

Task Answer your customer's questions about the prices for each of the specials.

MODELO   A — ¿Qué le puedo traer?

           B — Quisiera un café con leche, por favor.

               ¿Cuánto cuesta? *(How much does it cost?)*

           A — Un café con leche cuesta 250 pesetas.

           B — ¿Y cuánto cuesta un flan?

           A — Cuesta 600 pesetas.

Café de las Américas
Especiales del Día

Platos del día
- pollo asado   900 pts
- pescado con arroz
  y legumbres   1000 pts

Bebidas
- agua mineral   180 pts
- café   225 pts
- café con leche   250 pts
- refresco   250 pts

Entremeses
- ensalada mixta   500 pts
- ensalada de atún   600 pts

Postres
- helado   500 pts
- flan   600 pts

2. Now you're the customer. Ask what the prices are for the daily specials. Write the prices next to each special on the list below.

Café de las Américas
Especiales del Día

Platos del día
- arroz con pollo   _____
- camarones con bistec   _____

Bebidas
- jugo de naranja   300 pts
- café   _____
- café con leche   _____
- refresco   _____

Entremeses
- papas fritas   _____
- legumbres   _____

Postres
- helado   500 pts
- fruta   _____

If you have 2,000 pesetas to spend, what will you order and how much will you leave as a tip?

Voy a pedir _____ y _____ .

Y para tomar, quisiera _____ .

De propina voy a dejar _____ .

Who orders more food, you or your partner? _____

Who leaves a better tip? _____

Communicative Activity 8-3B

1. Situation You're a customer at a restaurant, and your partner is the waiter. You would like to order from the daily specials menu, but the items are listed without their prices.

Task Ask the waiter how much each item costs. Fill in the list of specials with the prices.

MODELO A — ¿Qué le puedo traer?

      B — Quisiera un café con leche, por favor.

        ¿Cuánto cuesta? *(How much does it cost?)*

      A — Un café con leche cuesta 250 pesetas.

      B — ¿Y cuánto cuesta un flan?

      A — Cuesta 600 pesetas.

Café de las Américas
Especiales del Día

Platos del día		**Bebidas**	
• pollo asado	_____	• agua mineral	_____
• pescado con arroz		• café	_____
y legumbres	_____	• café con leche	250 pts
		• refresco	_____
Entremeses		**Postres**	
• ensalada mixta	_____	• helado	_____
• ensalada de atún	_____	• flan	600 pts

2. Now you're the waiter. Answer your customer's questions about prices using the list below.

Café de las Américas
Especiales del Día

Platos del día		**Bebidas**	
• arroz con pollo	1100 pts	• jugo de naranja	300 pts
• camarones con		• café	225 pts
bistec	1300 pts	• café con leche	250 pts
		• refresco	250 pts
Entremeses		**Postres**	
• papas fritas	450 pts	• helado	500 pts
• legumbres	380 pts	• fruta	350 pts

If you have 2,000 pesetas to spend, what will you order and how much will you leave as a tip?

Voy a pedir _____ y _____.

Y para tomar, quisiera _____.

De propina voy a dejar _____.

Who orders more food, you or your partner? _____

Who leaves a better tip? _____

Communicative Activity 9-1A

1. Situation Your partner has just returned from shopping. You're curious about the gifts she or he bought.

Task Ask your partner questions about the following people and gifts. If you see a gift on the chart, ask who it's for; if you see a person, ask what gift your partner will give him or her.

MODELO   A — **¿Qué piensas regalarle a Joel?**
                     B — **Voy a regalarle una planta a Joel.**

MODELO   A — **¿A quién le vas a regalar un disco compacto?**
                     B — **Voy a regalarle un disco compacto a mi madre.**

Persona	Regalo
tu madre	un disco compacto
	una cartera
	unas corbatas
el profesor de inglés	
Ramona	
Joel	una planta

2. Now, answer your partner's questions about the following people and gifts.

MODELO   B — **¿Qué piensas regalarle a Ignacio?**
                     A — **Voy a regalarle unos dulces a Ignacio.**

MODELO   B — **¿A quién le vas a regalar una planta?**
                     A — **Voy a regalarle una planta a mi madre.**

Persona	Regalo
mi madre	una planta
mi abuelo	una corbata
Luis	unas flores
el profesor de inglés	una manzana
Ramona	un collar
Ignacio	unos dulces

Who do you think spent the most money buying gifts, you or your partner? Why?

_____

_____

Communicative Activity 9-1 B

1. Situation You've just returned from shopping. Your partner is curious about the gifts you've bought.

Task Answer your partner's questions about the following people and gifts.

MODELO   A — ¿Qué piensas regalarle a Joel?
          B — Voy a regalarle una planta a Joel.

MODELO   A — ¿A quién le vas a regalar un disco compacto?
          B — Voy a regalarle un disco compacto a mi madre.

Persona	Regalo
mi madre	un disco compacto
mi abuelo	una cartera
Luis	unas corbatas
el profesor de inglés	una tarjeta
Ramona	unos aretes
Joel	una planta

2. Now, ask your partner questions about the following people and gifts. If you see a gift on the chart, ask who it's for; if you see a person, ask what gift your partner will give him or her.

MODELO   B — ¿Qué piensas regalarle a Ignacio?
          A — Voy a regalarle unos dulces a Ignacio.

MODELO   B — ¿A quién le vas a regalar una planta?
          A — Voy a regalarle una planta a mi madre.

Persona	Regalo
tu madre	una planta
	una corbata
Luis	
	una manzana
Ramona	
Ignacio	unos dulces

Who do you think spent the most money buying gifts, you or your partner? Why?

_____

_____

Communicative Activity 9-2A

1. Situation It's August, and you have a job interview. Your best friend (your partner) is trying to help you decide what to wear.

Task Listen to your partner's suggestions and decide which clothes are appropriate for interviewing. Write your choices on the chart below.

MODELO **B — ¿Qué ropa vas a llevar a la entrevista *(interview)*?**
A — No sé. ¿Qué piensas?
B — ¿Por qué no llevas una camiseta de cuadros?
A — Bueno, no sé. or **¡Está bien!**

Choices

2. Your partner has been invited to a party. Suggest what she or he might wear from the choices on the chart below.

MODELO **A — ¿Qué ropa vas a llevar a la fiesta?**
B — No sé. ¿Qué piensas?
A — ¿Por qué no llevas una chaqueta gris?
B — ¡Prefiero llevar ropa cómoda!

Suggestions		
una camiseta de cuadros	una camiseta blanca	una camisa blanca
unos bluejeans unos pantalones negros	una falda negra unos pantalones cortos anaranjados	
un traje de baño	una chaqueta gris	un vestido de algodón
unos calcetines negros	unos calcetines de rayas	
un cinturón blanco	un cinturón de cuero negro	
unas botas verdes	unas sandalias	unos zapatos negros

What did you and your partner decide to wear? ______________________________

____

Communicative Activity 9-2B

1. **Situation** It's August, and your partner (your best friend) has a job interview. He or she is trying to decide what to wear.

   Task Try to help by suggesting the items listed on the chart below. Not all are appropriate!

   MODELO   B — ¿Qué ropa vas a llevar a la entrevista *(interview)*?
   A — No sé. ¿Qué piensas?
   B — ¿Por qué no llevas una camiseta de cuadros?
   A — Bueno, no sé.   or   ¡Está bien!

Suggestions		
una camiseta de cuadros	una camiseta blanca	una camisa blanca
unos bluejeans	una falda negra	
unos pantalones negros	unos pantalones cortos anaranjados	
un traje de baño	una chaqueta gris	un vestido de algodón
unos calcetines negros	unos calcetines de rayas	
un cinturón blanco	un cinturón de cuero negro	
unas botas verdes	unas sandalias	unos zapatos negros

2. You've been invited to a party. Ask your partner what you should wear. Choose the best suggestions and write them in the chart below.

   MODELO   A — ¿Qué ropa vas a llevar a la fiesta?
   B — No sé. ¿Qué piensas?
   A — ¿Por qué no llevas una chaqueta gris?
   B — ¡Prefiero llevar ropa cómoda!

Choices

What did you and your partner decide to wear? _____

_____

¡Ven conmigo! Level 1, Chapter 9

Communicative Activity 9-3A

1. Situation You work in a clothing store and your boss has asked you to investigate the competition's prices. Your partner works for a local competitor. Below you have a list of the prices your store charges for some items of clothing.

Task You go to your partner's store with a list of clothing and prices. Find out how much your partner's store charges for these items.

MODELO   A — ¿Cuánto cuestan los bluejeans?
               B — Cuestan veintiocho dólares con cincuenta centavos.

Mi tienda		La competencia *(competition)*
bluejeans	$37.79	*$28.50*
camisetas	$15.99	_____
pantalones cortos	$8.00	_____
chaquetas	$89.99	_____
calcetines (paquete de 3)	$5.99	_____
las sandalias	$41.50	_____

2. Now, switch roles. Your partner wants to make a similar comparison. Answer his or her questions about a different list of clothing and prices.

MODELO   B — ¿Cuánto cuesta un vestido?
               A — Cuesta cincuenta y nueve dólares.

Mi tienda	
camisas	$42.00
faldas	$27.60
traje de baño	$19.50
vestido	$59.00
zapatos de tenis	$78.69
el cinturón de cuero	$18.00

Now, compare your lists. Which items are more expensive at your store? At your partner's store? Where would you prefer to shop? Why?

_____

_____

◈ **Communicative Activity 9-3B**

COMMUNICATIVE ACTIVITIES

1. **Situation** You work in a clothing store and your boss has asked you to investigate the competition's prices. Your partner works for a local competitor. Below you have a list of the prices your store charges for some items of clothing.

Task Answer your partner's questions about the clothing prices at your store.

MODELO   A — ¿Cuánto cuestan los bluejeans?
           B — Cuestan veintiocho dólares con cincuenta centavos.

Mi tienda	
bluejeans	$28.50
camisetas	$10.75
pantalones cortos	$17.00
chaquetas	$39.99
calcetines (paquete de 3)	$8.99
las sandalias	$46.00

2. Now, switch roles. You go to your partner's store with a list of clothing and prices. Find out how much your partner's store charges for these items.

MODELO   B — ¿Cuánto cuesta un vestido?
           A — Cuesta cincuenta y nueve dólares.

Mi tienda		La competencia *(competition)*
camisas	$37.00	_____
faldas	$20.00	_____
traje de baño	$49.50	_____
vestido	$129.00	*$59.00*
zapatos de tenis	$37.88	_____
el cinturón de cuero	$22.50	_____

Now, compare your lists. Which items are more expensive at your store? At your partner's store? Where would you prefer to shop? Why?

_____

_____

Communicative Activity 10-1A

1. Situation Your partner's friend Silvia is giving her **quinceañera** party right now. Your partner is already at the party, but you are not sure if you want to go. You're talking to him or her on the phone.

Task Ask your partner what's going on at the party and what the following people are doing, and then decide if you want to go.

MODELO   A — ¿Qué está haciendo Carlos en la fiesta?
               B — Bueno, Carlos está bailando con Nuria.

Persona	¿Qué está haciendo?
Ben	
Mariana	
Doug	
Yolanda	
Nuria	
Carlos	está bailando con Nuria
Pablo	

2. Now switch roles. You're at Catalina's birthday party and your partner is trying to decide whether he or she wants to come. Answer your partner's questions about what's going on at the party so he or she can decide.

MODELO   B — ¿Qué está haciendo Mónica en la fiesta?
               A — Mónica está escuchando a Federico.

Imagine what the people are like at the two parties. Which party would you rather attend, and why?

_____

COMMUNICATIVE ACTIVITIES

Communicative Activity 10-1B

1. Situation Your friend Silvia is giving her **quinceañera** party right now. You're at the party already, but your partner is not sure that she or he wants to go. You're talking to her or him on the phone.

Task Answer your partner's questions about what's going on at the party so she or he can decide whether to come.

MODELO   A — ¿Qué está haciendo Carlos en la fiesta?
                B — Bueno, Carlos está bailando con Nuria.

2. Now switch roles. Your classmate Catalina is having a birthday party right now. Your partner is already at the party, but you're not sure whether you want to go. You're talking to your partner on the phone. Ask him or her what's going on at the party and what the following people are doing, and then decide if you want to go.

MODELO   B — ¿Qué está haciendo Mónica en la fiesta?
                A — Mónica está escuchando a Federico.

Persona	¿Qué está haciendo?
Mónica	está escuchando a Federico
Adriana	
Federico	
Celia	
Pepe	
Bernardo	
Linda	

Imagine what the people are like at the two parties. Which party would you rather attend, and why?

_____

Nombre _____ Clase _____ Fecha _____

1. Situation You and your partner are siblings. You work together in your parents' restaurant. At the end of each night, several things have to be done before you close.

Task You ask what needs to be done, and your partner answers with an informal command.

MODELO   A — ¿Qué necesito hacer?
             B — Bueno, pasa la aspiradora en el comedor.
             A — De acuerdo. or Está bien.

	Task
1	pasar la aspiradora en el comedor (*dining room*)
2	
3	
4	
5	
6	
7	
8	
9	

2. Now, imagine that your partner is an older restaurant worker. You ask your partner politely to do all the tasks that your "sibling" had you do in part 1, but he or she declines.

MODELO   A — Don Luis, ¿me hace el favor de pasar la aspiradora en el comedor?
             B — Lo siento, pero en este momento...

Which task(s) could you postpone until the next morning? Why?

_____

_____

HRW material copyrighted under notice appearing earlier in this work.

COMMUNICATIVE ACTIVITIES

Communicative Activity 10-2B

1. **Situation** You and your partner are siblings. You work together in your parents' restaurant. At the end of each night, several things have to be done before you close the restaurant.

   Task Your partner asks what needs to be done, and you answer with an informal command.

   MODELO   A — ¿Qué necesito hacer?
   B — Bueno, pasa la aspiradora en el comedor.
   A — De acuerdo. or Está bien.

	Task
1	pasar la aspiradora en el comedor (*dining room*)
2	lavar los platos
3	poner los platos en el gabinete
4	limpiar la cocina
5	sacar la basura
6	trapear (*mop*) el suelo de la cocina
7	limpiar los baños
8	contar la caja (*cash register*)
9	poner las mesas para mañana

2. Now, imagine that you are an older restaurant worker. Your partner asks you politely to do all the tasks that you told your "sibling" to do in part 1, but you are unwilling. You decline.

   MODELO   A — Don Luis, ¿me hace el favor de pasar la aspiradora en el comedor?
   B — Lo siento, pero en este momento...

   Which task(s) could you postpone until the next morning? Why?

   _____

   _____

¡Ven conmigo! Level 1, Chapter 10

Communicative Activity 10-3A

1. Situation You and your partner are in a musical play together, and you missed last night's rehearsal.

Task Ask your partner for information about the rehearsal and fill in the chart.

MODELO   A — ¿A qué hora empezaron ustedes?
          B — Empezamos a las siete.

El ensayo
¿A qué hora empezaron ustedes? a las siete
¿Dónde ensayaron (*did you rehearse*) ustedes?
¿Quiénes participaron?
¿Quién cantó más?
¿Qué hiciste tú?
¿A qué hora terminaron ustedes?

2. You and your partner usually study with a group of students, but your partner missed the group since she or he went to rehearsal. Answer her or his questions about what happened at the study group, based on the chart below.

MODELO   B — ¿A qué hora empezaron ustedes?
          A — Empezamos a las siete.

El grupo de estudiar
empezar / 7:00 p.m.
estudiar / en casa de Jorge
participar / Jorge, tú, Mariela, Bernardo y yo
practicar / el vocabulario
yo / preparar un diálogo en español
Mariela / no hacer nada

Do you think it was more important to go to rehearsal or to study with your friends last night? Why?

_____

Communicative Activity 10-3B

1. Situation You and your partner are in a musical play together, and your partner missed last night's rehearsal.

Task Answer your partner's questions about the rehearsal.

MODELO   A — ¿A qué hora empezaron ustedes?
                B — Empezamos a las siete.

El ensayo
empezar / 7:00
ensayar (*to rehearse*) / la cafetería
participar / Claudia, Jaime, Guillermo, Pepe, Sandra y yo
Jaime / cantar
yo / bailar
terminar / 9:45

2. You and your partner usually study with a group of students. You didn't study last night, since you went to rehearsal. Find out what happened.

MODELO   B — ¿A qué hora empezaron ustedes?
                A — Empezamos a las siete.

El grupo de estudiar
¿A qué hora empezaron ustedes? a las siete
¿Dónde estudiaron ustedes?
¿Quiénes participaron?
¿Qué practicaron?
¿Qué hiciste tú?
¿Quién no hizo nada?

Do you think it was more important to go to rehearsal or to study with your friends last night? Why?

_____

Communicative Activity 11-1A

1. Situation You're a trainer at the health club where your partner has just become a member. You need to ask him or her for some information before he or she can begin an exercise program.

Task Ask your partner questions and mark the answers on the information sheet below.

MODELO   A — ¿Qué tomas con frecuencia?
          B — Yo tomo café.

Bebidas		Comidas	
(√) café	( ) jugo de fruta	( ) pizza	( ) pescado
( ) agua	( ) leche	( ) hamburguesas	( ) ensalada
( ) refrescos		y papas fritas	( ) chocolate
		( ) verduras	
Pasatiempos		**Ejercicios**	
( ) escuchar música	( ) jugar deportes	( ) levantar pesas	( ) hacer yoga
( ) mirar la televisión	( ) bailar	( ) patinar	( ) caminar
( ) montar a caballo	( ) leer	( ) hacer ejercicios aeróbicos	( ) correr

2. Now, you want to join an exercise program. Answer the health club trainer's questions according to the information sheet.

MODELO   B — ¿Qué tomas con frecuencia?
          A — Yo tomo agua.

Bebidas		Comidas	
( ) café	( ) jugo de fruta	( ) pizza	(√) pescado
(√) agua	(√) leche	( ) hamburguesas	(√) ensalada
( ) refrescos		y papas fritas	( ) chocolate
		(√) verduras	
Pasatiempos		**Ejercicios**	
(√) escuchar música	( ) jugar deportes	( ) levantar pesas	(√) hacer yoga
( ) mirar la televisión	( ) bailar	( ) patinar	( ) caminar
(√) montar a caballo	( ) leer	( ) hacer ejercicios aeróbicos	( ) correr

As a trainer, what advice would you give to each person?

_____

_____

Communicative Activity 11-1B

1. Situation You've just joined a health club. Before you can join an exercise program, your trainer asks you for some information.

Task Answer your trainer's questions according to the information sheet below.

MODELO   A — ¿Qué tomas con frecuencia?
                B — Yo tomo café.

Bebidas		Comidas	
(√) café	( ) jugo de fruta	(√) pizza	( ) pescado
( ) agua	( ) leche	(√) hamburguesas	( ) ensalada
( ) refrescos		y papas fritas	(√) chocolate
		( ) verduras	
Pasatiempos		**Ejercicios**	
( ) escuchar música	( ) jugar deportes	( ) levantar pesas	( ) hacer yoga
(√) mirar la televisión	( ) bailar	( ) patinar	( ) caminar
( ) montar a caballo	(√) leer	(√) hacer ejercicios aeróbicos	( ) correr

2. Now, you're the health club trainer. Ask your partner questions and mark the information below.

MODELO   B — ¿Qué tomas con frecuencia?
                A — Yo tomo agua.

Bebidas		Comidas	
( ) café	( ) jugo de fruta	( ) pizza	( ) pescado
(√) agua	( ) leche	( ) hamburguesas	( ) ensalada
( ) refrescos		y papas fritas	( ) chocolate
		( ) verduras	
Pasatiempos		**Ejercicios**	
( ) escuchar música	( ) jugar deportes	( ) levantar pesas	( ) hacer yoga
( ) mirar la televisión	( ) bailar	( ) patinar	( ) caminar
( ) montar a caballo	( ) leer	( ) hacer ejercicios aeróbicos	( ) correr

As a trainer, what advice would you give to each person?

_____

_____

Nombre _____ Clase _____ Fecha _____

1. **Situation** It's Saturday afternoon and you're bored. You want one of your friends to go to the movies with you, but everyone seems to be complaining about how they feel.

   Task Your partner will play the role of each of your friends. When your friend answers the phone, ask how he or she is feeling. Note the answer by each person's name.

   MODELO   B — ¿Aló?
              A — Hola, Tomás. ¿Cómo estás?
              B — Estoy nervioso.
              A — ¿Por qué?
              B — Pues, ...

Tomás

Números de Teléfono

Nombre : _Tomás_
Tel : _899-6373_

Nombre : _Lupita_
Tel : _314-3795_

Nombre : _Juan_
Tel : _466-0285_

Nombre : _Alicia_
Tel : _798-1115_

Nombre : _Marco_
Tel : _455-4224_

Nombre : _____
Tel : _____

Tomás – No puede. Está nervioso.
Lupita –

2. Now, change roles. Answer the phone and then answer your partner's questions according to the picture of each person below.

   MODELO   A — ¿Aló?
              B — Hola, Linda. ¿Cómo te sientes?
              A — Me duele el pie.
              B — ¿Qué te pasa?
              A — Pues, ...

Linda

Midori   **Joe**   **Deidre**   **Jeff**

Compare your list of friends' complaints with your partner's. Which friends from either list do you think might be able to go to the movies with you?

Communicative Activity 11-2B

1. Situation It's Saturday afternoon and your partner is bored. He or she wants someone to go to the movies, but everyone seems to be complaining about how they feel.

Task Your partner will phone and ask how you're feeling. Use the photos below to help you with your answers.

MODELO   B — ¿Aló?
               A — Hola, Tomás. ¿Cómo estás?
               B — Estoy nervioso.
               A — ¿Por qué?
               B — Pues, ...

Tomás

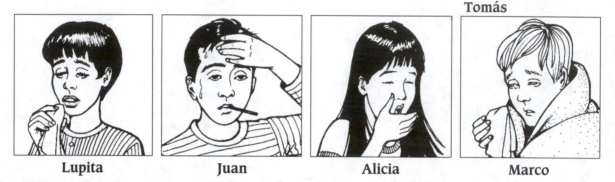

Lupita   Juan   Alicia   Marco

2. Now, change roles. Call the friends on your list and, when they answer, ask how they're feeling. Note their answers by each of their names.

MODELO   A — ¿Aló?
               B — Hola, Linda. ¿Cómo te sientes?
               A — Me duele el pie.
               B — ¿Qué te pasa?
               A — Pues, ...

Linda

Números de Teléfono

Nombre : _Linda_
Tel : _354-3079_

Nombre : _Midori_
Tel : _533-1728_

Nombre : _Joe_
Tel : _454-1572_

Nombre : _Deidre_
Tel : _377-1492_

Nombre : _Jeff_
Tel : _215-9208_

Nombre : _____
Tel : _____

Linda – No puede.
*   Le duele el pie.*

Midori –

Compare your list of friends' complaints with your partner's. Which friends from either list do you think might be able to go to the movies with you?

1. **Situation** It's Sunday night and your partner has just returned from San Juan, Puerto Rico. You call your partner to find out what she or he did while on vacation.

Task Ask your partner what she or he did during the week and when. Take notes on her or his answers so you can compare your activities.

MODELO   A — ¿Qué hiciste el lunes pasado?
B — Fui a la Plaza de Armas.

lunes	martes	miércoles	jueves	viernes	sábado
Ir a la Plaza de Armas					
					domingo

2. Now answer your partner's questions about what you did during the week your partner was away and you were at home.

MODELO   B — ¿Qué hiciste el lunes pasado?
A — Fui al centro.

lunes	martes	miércoles	jueves	viernes	sábado
Ir al centro	11:00 a.m. Limpiar el cuarto	9:00 a.m. Jugar al tenis	2:30 p.m. Montar a caballo	8:00 p.m. Cenar en el restaurante	6:30 p.m. Ir al cine
					domingo

Which activities did you and your partner have in common during the week?

_____

COMMUNICATIVE ACTIVITIES

Communicative Activity 11-3B

1. **Situation** It's Sunday night and you have just returned this afternoon from San Juan, Puerto Rico. Your friend calls because he or she wants to know what you did and when.

   Task Answer your partner's questions about what you did on your vacation.

   MODELO   A — ¿Qué hiciste el lunes pasado?
              B — Fui a la Plaza de Armas.

lunes	martes	miércoles	jueves	viernes	sábado
Ir a la Plaza de Armas	8:00 a.m. Jugar al tenis	3:00 p.m. Visitar el Castillo del Morro	10:00 a.m. Caminar por la Calle de Cristo	5:00 p.m. Ir a la playa	9:00 p.m. Cenar en el restaurante

domingo
8:30 p.m. Regresar a casa

2. Now ask your partner what he or she did at home during the week while you were gone. Take notes on his or her answers so you can compare your activities.

   MODELO   B — ¿Qué hiciste el lunes pasado?
              A — Fui al centro.

lunes	martes	miércoles	jueves	viernes	sábado
Ir al centro					

domingo

   Which activities did you and your partner have in common during the week?

   _____

   _____

Communicative Activity 12-1A

1. Situation You and your partner are evaluating the applications of candidates for president of the Panamerican Club next year. You want to find out what the candidates like to do for fun and what their plans are for the summer.

Task From the list of names below, ask your partner what the following candidates like to do for fun on the weekends and what they want to do this summer.

MODELO   A — ¿Qué hace Dinora Periko los fines de semana?
                B — Primero va a la biblioteca, después regresa a casa, hace la tarea y luego mira la televisión.
                A — ¿Qué piensa hacer este verano?
                B — Espera leer mucho y quiere ir a Argentina.

• C A N D I D A T O S •	N O T A S
Dinora Periko Lucas Valladolid Campos Ensoñación Lowemberg	

2. Now switch roles and answer your partner's questions about the candidates. Unfortunately, you've lost the original applications and can only answer by looking at the notes you took during the oral interviews of the candidates.

MODELO   B — ¿Qué hace Mónica Ibáñez los fines de semana?
                A — Primero visita a sus primos, después va al centro comercial y luego juega al béisbol.
                B — ¿Qué piensa hacer este verano?
                A — Espera practicar la natación y quiere trabajar.

Candidato	Fines de semana	Planes para el verano
Mónica Ibáñez	visitar primos, ir al centro comercial, jugar al béisbol	practicar la natación, trabajar
Doroteo Santander Lino	descansar, salir con los amigos, jugar al fútbol	esquiar, ir a Colorado
Juan José Ambriz Flores	pasear con el perro, quedarse con los abuelos, hacer ejercicios en el gimnasio	descansar en la playa, vivir en México por dos meses

Which of the candidates will you and your partner recommend? _____

Why? _____

COMMUNICATIVE ACTIVITIES

Communicative Activity 12-1D

1. Situation You and your partner are evaluating the applications of candidates for president of the Panamerican Club next year. Your partner wants to find out what the candidates like to do for fun and what their plans are for the summer. Unfortunately, you've lost the original applications and can only answer his or her questions by looking at the notes you took during the oral interviews of the candidates.

Task Answer your partner's questions about the candidates.

MODELO
A — ¿Qué hace Dinora Periko los fines de semana?
B — Primero va a la biblioteca, después regresa a casa, hace la tarea y luego mira la televisión.
A — ¿Qué piensa hacer este verano?
B — Espera leer mucho y quiere ir a Argentina.

Candidato	Fines de semana	Planes para el verano
Dinora Periko	ir a la biblioteca, regresar a casa, mirar la televisión	leer mucho, ir a Argentina
Lucas Valladolid Campos	pescar, nadar, jugar al basquetbol	hacer yoga, levantar pesas
Ensoñación Lowemberg	desayunar en la cafetería, correr en el parque, ir a conciertos	viajar a Canadá, esquiar en las montañas

2. Now, switch roles and ask your partner questions about your list of candidates.

MODELO
B — ¿Qué hace Mónica Ibáñez los fines de semana?
A — Primero visita a sus primos, después va al centro comercial, y luego juega al béisbol.
B — ¿Qué piensa hacer este verano?
A — Espera practicar la natación y quiere trabajar.

• C A N D I D A T O S •	N O T A S
Mónica Ibáñez	
Doroteo Santander Lino	
Juan José Ambriz Flores	

Which of the candidates will you and your partner recommend? _____

Why? _____

1. **Situation** You and your partner are designing the ideal vacation for some of your relatives. You've written down information about their interests, including what they'd like to do on vacation. Your partner has a list of ideal destinations.

Task Match each of your relatives with the destination that best meets his or her needs.

MODELO   A — A mi tía Magdalena le gustaría visitar museos y ver momumentos históricos europeos. Ella sólo habla español.
               B — Ella puede ir a España.

Pariente	Preferencias	Destino
tía Magdalena	visitar museos, ver monumentos históricos europeos; sólo habla español	España
abuelo Luis	hacer turismo, practicar el alemán	
hermana Mónica	tomar el sol en la playa, dar caminatas en la selva; le encantan las islas	
primo Sergio	ir de compras, ir de vela, tomar el sol en la playa; también le gusta la comida cubana	
sobrina Juanita	visitar museos europeos, montar en bicicleta, practicar el inglés	
tío Miguel	visitar museos, escalar montañas, ver ruinas de los Inca	

2. Now switch roles. Below you have a list of more destinations. Help your partner match his or her relatives with their ideal destination.

MODELO   B — A mi abuela Delia le gustaría hacer turismo y ver la gran muralla.
               A — Ella puede ir a China.

> **Destinos más deseados de este año**
>
> Egipto
> Francia
> México
> San Antonio, Texas
> Italia
> China
> Costa Rica

Which of all the relatives, yours and your partner's, do both of you think will have the best vacation?

_____ Why? _____

Communicative Activity 12-2B

1. Situation You and your partner are designing the ideal vacation for some of his or her relatives. He or she has written down information about their interests, including what they'd like to do on vacation.

Task Match each of his or her relatives with a destination on your list.

MODELO   A — A mi tía Magdalena le gustaría visitar museos y ver momumentos históricos europeos. Ella sólo habla español.
                 B — Ella puede ir a España.

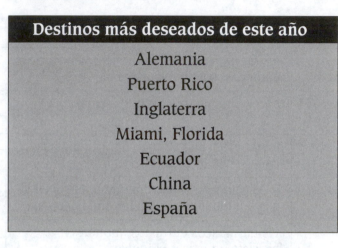

Destinos más deseados de este año

Alemania
Puerto Rico
Inglaterra
Miami, Florida
Ecuador
China
España

2. Now switch roles. Match your relatives with your partner's list of ideal destinations.

MODELO   B — A mi abuela Delia le gustaría hacer turismo y ver la gran muralla.
                 A — Ella puede ir a China.

Pariente	Preferencias	Destino
abuela Delia	hacer turismo, ver la Gran Muralla *(Great Wall)*	China
primo Martín	ver los museos de arte, comer buena comida, practicar el francés	
cuñada Patricia	explorar las grandes ciudades, visitar los museos, ver las ruinas aztecas	
tía Ana	ver las pirámides, explorar el desierto	
hermano Vicente	visitar los museos, tomar el sol, practicar el italiano	
hermana Alicia	comer comida mexicana, ir a un rodeo; habla español, pero quiere practicar el inglés	

Which of all the relatives, yours and your partner's, do both of you think will have the best vacation?

_____ Why? _____

Communicative Activity 12-3A

1. Situation You and your partner are agents tracking two international spies. Your partner has followed them to a number of European countries, but they caught on to him or her and got away.

Task Use the decoding form below to ask your partner what the spies did and where. Then unscramble the circled letters to find the name of the country where they might be hiding now.

MODELO
A — ¿En qué país sacaron muchas fotos?
B — Sacaron muchas fotos en Italia.

CASO DE ESPIONAJE No. 148872-X
Código para resolver el paradero (whereabouts) de los espías internacionales:

1. País donde sacaron muchas fotos   I t a l i a
2. País donde fueron de vela   __ __ __ __ __ __
3. País donde saltaron en paracaídas   __ __ __ __ __ __ __ __ __
4. País donde tomaron el sol   __ __ __ __ __ __
5. País donde montaron en bicicleta   __ __ __ __ __ __ __ __
6. País donde escalaron montañas   __ __ __ __ __ __ __

---

2. To your surprise, you've realized the spies have been doing the same things in Latin America. Looking at your own photographs, answer your partner's questions to help him or her decode the name of the country which might be the spies' new hideout.

MODELO
B— ¿En qué país escalaron montañas?
A — Escalaron montañas en Bolivia.

Bolivia   Venezuela   México   Honduras   Colombia

Which are the two countries where they could be hiding now?

_____ and _____

COMMUNICATIVE ACTIVITIES

Communicative Activity 12-3B

1. Situation You and your partner are agents tracking two international spies. You followed them to a number of European countries, but they caught on to you and got away.

Task Use the photos you took to answer your partner's questions about the spies' activities.

MODELO   A — ¿En qué país sacaron muchas fotos?
          B — Sacaron muchas fotos en Italia.

Inglaterra

España

Italia

Alemania

Portugal

Francia

2. To your surprise, your partner has realized that he's been tracking the same spies through Latin America and they've been doing the same things. Based on the decoding form below, ask your partner what the spies did in each Latin American country. Then unscramble the circled letters to find the location of the spies' new international hideout.

MODELO   B— ¿En qué país escalaron montañas?
          A — Escalaron montañas en Bolivia.

CASO DE ESPIONAJE No. 148872-Y
Código para resolver el paradero (whereabouts) de los espías internacionales:

1. País donde escalaron montañas   B o (l) i v i a

2. País donde fueron de vela   (○) __ __ __ __ __

3. País donde tomaron el sol   __ __ __ __ (○) __ __

4. País donde sacaron muchas fotos   __ __ __ __ __ (○) __

5. País donde saltaron en paracaídas   __ (○) __ __ __ __ __

Which are the two countries where they could be hiding now?

_____ and _____

Realia and Suggestions
For Using Realia

Illustration and text adapted from "Cita a Ciegas" from *Ragazza*, no. 91, May 1997.
Copyright © 1997 by *Hachette Filipacchi.* Reprinted by permission of the publisher.

Realia 1-2

SOLICITUD DE PASAPORTE

RADICAL	NÚMERO	AÑO

CLASE
☐ I ☐ E ☐ C

SERIE NÚMERO

FOTOS

EXCMO. SEÑOR:

TITULAR

NOMBRE: ROSA MARÍA

APELLIDO 1: ROMERO

APELLIDO 2: BARREIRO

D.N.I.: 33.260.717

SEXO: F

PROFESIÓN:

ESTADO CIVIL: SOLTERA

LUGAR DE NACIMIENTO: SANTIAGO

PROVINCIA NACIMIENTO: LA CORUÑA

CLAVE:

F. NACIMIENTO: 28, X, 62

NOMBRE DEL PADRE: VENTURA

NOMBRE DE LA MADRE: MARÍA

DOMICILIO

CALLE O PLAZA: EDUARDO PONDAL

Nº: 24

D.P.:

LOCALIDAD: SANTIAGO

PROVINCIA: LA CORUÑA

CLAVE:

SOLICITUD DE PASAPORTE

RADICAL	NÚMERO	AÑO

CLASE
☐ I ☐ E ☐ C

SERIE NÚMERO

FOTOS

EXCMO. SEÑOR:

TITULAR

NOMBRE:

APELLIDO 1:

APELLIDO 2:

D.N.I.:

SEXO:

PROFESIÓN:

ESTADO CIVIL:

LUGAR DE NACIMIENTO:

PROVINCIA NACIMIENTO:

CLAVE:

F. NACIMIENTO:

NOMBRE DEL PADRE:

NOMBRE DE LA MADRE:

DOMICILIO

CALLE O PLAZA:

Nº:

D.P.:

LOCALIDAD:

PROVINCIA:

CLAVE:

REALIA

¿Os gusta el colegio?

el gran debate

En cada número, uno de vosotros plantea una pregunta. Los lectores y las lectoras responden dando su opinión. Ésta es la pregunta de Fernando, de Murcia.

"¿Os gusta el colegio?"
Fernando, Murcia

"¿Os gusta el colegio? ¡A mí me encanta! Aunque tenga que hacer redacciones y deberes y aunque tenga que madrugar, me encanta. ¿Y a vosotros?"

"Tengo ganas de volver"
Cristina, Huesca

"A mí también me gusta mucho el colegio, como a Fernando. Cuando los padres de un amigo o una amiga me dicen delante de él o de ella si tengo ganas de volver al colegio, yo digo que sí, aunque después mis amigos se suelen reír de mí. Además, voy muy bien en clase, y me dicen que quiero ir porque no tengo problemas en aprobar. Pero, por una parte, este año no me apetece mucho ir porque empiezo 1° de ESO y llevaré un horario muy malo, teniendo que madrugar. Pero si se ríen de tus ganas de ir al colegio, no hagas caso, se sentirán ignorados y te dejarán de molestar."

"Nos prepara para el futuro"
Jordi, Barcelona

"Yo soy de la misma opinión que Fernando. Y aunque no te guste, tu futuro depende del colegio. Para mí el colegio es una especie de preparación para el día de mañana. Nos enseña el camino de nuestro futuro."

"Tienes tu recompensa"
Isabel, Madrid

"¡Me encanta, Fernando! Muchas veces hay que hacer bastantes deberes o se te acumulan todos los exámenes y no puedes más, pero te enseñan muchas cosas nuevas e interesantes y a veces divertidas. Además, luego, al final de curso, por haberte esforzado tanto tienes tu recompensa y tus padres se alegran mucho."

Sabiondy   Tapón   Modelna   Pancho   Pitagorín   Gallito

REALIA

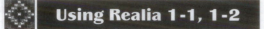

Realia 1-1: Telephone Conversation

1. **Reading:** Have students look for clues about what might be going on in the scene. Is Cristián happy to be speaking to Clara? How do you know?

2. **Listening:** Read the dialogue out loud, changing your voice for the different characters, and ask students to identify the speaker (Clara or Cristián). Note that there are three lines each per character.

3. **Writing:** Have students write a similar dialogue that they might have when calling a friend.

4. **Pair work/Speaking:** Have students work with a partner to act out the dialogue they each wrote for number 3.

5. **Culture:** You might point out that the way Spanish-speakers answer the phone varies from country to country. In Spain they use **¡Diga!**, in Mexico **¡Bueno!**, and in Argentina **¡Aló!**

Realia 1-2: Passport applications

1. **Speaking:** Ask students what this form is for. Why might someone need a passport?

2. **Listening:** Tell students that this passport application is from Spain. You may want to go over the meaning of any unfamiliar terms: **D.N.I., estado civil, provincia de nacimiento, nº, localidad,** and **provincia. D.N.I.** stands for **documento nacional de identidad**, the Spanish equivalent of a Social Security card. Spain is divided into regions and provinces (**provincias**) instead of states and counties; **nº** is the Spanish abbreviation for **número**; and **localidad** means *town* or *city*.

3. **Reading:** Have students read the information on the filled-out application and give five facts about the applicant.

4. **Writing:** Have students fill out the blank application or supply the information on a blank sheet of paper. They may use the completed application as a guide.

5. **Group work/Speaking:** Divide the class into groups of two or three. Have students ask one another questions and use the information to fill out the blank form.

6. **Culture:** You might point out that in Spanish-speaking countries people use two last names instead of one. The first **apellido** *(last name)* comes from the father and the second comes from the mother. The most common last names are: Pérez, García, Rodríguez, Rivera, Sánchez, and López. The **-ez** suffix in Spanish last names indicates a patronymic surname (derived from the father's name), such as Pérez from Pedro, Sánchez from Sancho, López from Lope, and Rodríguez from Rodrigo. Ask students if they know any other patronymic names.

Realia 1-3: Article: ¿Os gusta el colegio?

1. **Reading:** Have students skim the article looking for Chapter 1 **Vocabulario**. List the words and phrases on the board. (**me encanta, mucho, muchas, me gusta mucho, un amigo, amiga, clase, mañana**) You may want to go over the meaning of some unfamiliar terms, such as **colegio** *(high school)*, **plantea** *(states)*, **madrugar** *(to get up early)*, **se suelen reír** *(they often laugh at me)*, **no me apetece mucho** *(I don't care much for)*, **molestar** *(to annoy)*, **por haberte esforzado** *(for having made the effort)*. However, emphasize that it is possible to get the gist of a reading without knowing all the words.

2. **Listening:** Read the article aloud in sections, pausing to ask students the following questions: What expressions of liking or disliking did they hear? What did each person like or dislike?

3. **Writing/Speaking:** Divide the class into groups of three. Have students work together to write a letter to a friend about their likes and dislikes. Have them use words and phrases from the **Vocabulario** on page 4 of the *Pupil's Edition*, and the letter in the **fotonovela** on page 19. Each group should be prepared to read the letter to the class.

4. **Culture:** Explain to students that the use of the indirect object pronoun form **os** in the title refers to the plural "you" form (**vosotros**) used almost exclusively in Spain. Point out that this article is reprinted from a Spanish magazine for young teens. The cartoon characters represent student mascots for this magazine. Have them look on a map of Spain to find where each student quoted is from. (Murcia, Madrid, Huesca and Barcelona)

REALIA

¡Ven conmigo! Level 1, Chapter 1   Activities for Communication   **79**

HRW material copyrighted under notice appearing earlier in this work.

Realia 2-1

¡Ven conmigo! Level 1, Chapter 2

Illustration and text adapted from Advertisement for "**Mueblerías Berríos**", Caguas, Puerto Rico, June 1997. Reprinted by permission of the *Mueblerías Berríos*.

Text and illustrations, "Laura Ser O No Ser" from *Ahora*, vol. 4, no. 1, September/October 1997. Copyright © 1997 by *Scholastic Inc.* Reprinted by permission of the publisher.

Realia 2-1: School supply ad

1. **Reading/Speaking:** Ask students about the prices in the ad. How do the prices compare to the cost of those items in the United States? Explain that the prices shown are in **pesetas**, the currency of Spain. Have students look up the exchange rate for the **peseta** in a newspaper and convert the prices to dollars. Are the items advertised expensive, inexpensive, or comparably priced to similar items where you live? Ask students if the items advertised are items they would buy.

2. **Reading:** Ask students to scan the ad for cognates and list them on the board or on a transparency. Then ask them what they think the small graphics at the bottom of the advertisement represent. If they don't guess correctly, tell them what services these graphics represent.

3. **Group work/Writing:** Have students work in groups to create their own school supply ad. Bring in ads and have students cut out items and write the text to accompany each in Spanish. Have them assign realistic prices in **pesetas** or **euros.**

4. **Culture:** Explain that clothing and shoe sizes abroad are not the same as in the United States. Shoe sizes are given using the metric system. If a shopper can't remember what size he or she needs, the clerk can always help. **¿Qué número/talla necesito?** *(What size do I need?)* You may ask your students to look at the following chart and find the size of shoes they wear.

Zapatos en:	USA	METRIC SYSTEM
	7	40
	8	41
	9	43
	10	44
	12	45

Realia 2-2: Ad for bedroom furniture

1. **Speaking:** Ask students **¿Qué hay en el cuarto?** Have them identify the different items in the ad using the vocabulary they have learned in this chapter. (**silla, cama, lámpara, ventana, escritorio, reloj, revista, libro, bolígrafo, lápiz**)

2. **Reading:** Have students scan the ad for cognates and list them on the board or on an overhead transparency. Encourage students to guess the meaning of words based on their context. Explain any unfamiliar words, such as: **una plaza** *(twin)*, **dos plazas** *(full)*, **tablillero** *(bookshelves)*, **mensual** *(monthly)*, **gavetas** *(drawers)*, **mesa de noche** *(night stand)*, and the abbreviation **disp. [disponible]** *(available)*

3. **Writing:** Have students write their own ads for a furniture store featuring what they would have in their ideal rooms. They should include prices.

4. **Speaking:** Have students present their ads to the class in the style of a television commercial for a furniture store or of a human interest feature on a celebrity's home. They should describe the contents of the room and say how many pieces of furniture are in it. You may want to videotape these presentations.

5. **Culture:** Point out to students that since this ad is from Puerto Rico, English words are mixed in with the Spanish, as is often the case in informal contexts. Ask students how many different payment plans the store offers. (**crédito, cash, mensual**)

Realia 2-3: Laura Cartoon

1. **Reading:** First have students look at the pictures and guess what the cartoon is about, without reading any words. Ask them to look for any words or expressions that "stand out" and hypothesize why the artist emphasized those. Remind students that they can often tell what a passage is about without reading every word, and can guess the meaning of words by the drawings. Examples you might point out are **espejo, pie derecho,** and **autobús.** Then ask them to scan for cognates (**amuleto, humor, horrible, vacaciones, normal, obligatorio, instituto**), and known vocabulary. (**el primer día de clases, buenos días, hola**)

2. **Listening:** Read the cartoon aloud to the class, pausing between frames. You may want to do this as a dictation, with the students' cartoons covered, and then have them check their spelling.

3. **Writing:** Have students form small groups. They should work together to write alternate captions for the speech bubbles of the cartoon, using the **Vocabulario** from *Pupil's Edition*, page 65.

4. **Speaking/Listening:** Have each group read a portion of their original captions. Students should listen for the gist and answer simple comprehension questions you ask based on the content of each group's work.

5. **Culture:** Point out that families in Spanish-speaking countries often do not own more than one car. Therefore, teenagers either walk or take the bus to where they need to go.

UNIDAD EDUCATIVA ACADEMIA WASHINGTON

GRADO ___9no___

HORA	LUNES	MARTES	MIÉRCOLES	JUEVES	VIERNES
7:30–8:15	FÍSICA	GEOGRAF. VENEZIA.	GEOGRAF. VENZLA.	FÍSICA	CASTELLANO
8:15–9:00	INGLÉS	GEOGRAF. VENEZIA.	FÍSICA	INGLÉS	CASTELLANO/COMP
9:00–9:45	QUÍMICA	MATEMÁTICA	QUÍMICA	CAT. BOLIVAR	GUIATURA
9:55–10:40	QUÍMICA	MATEMÁTICA	CASTELLANO	QUÍMICA	ED. FÍSICA/AT
10:40–11:25	TRICOL/INGLÉS	FÍSICA	GEOGRAF. VENEZLA.	MATEMÁTICA	INGLÉS
11:25–12:10	INGLÉS/TRICOL.	BIOLOGÍA	CASTELLANO	MATEMÁTICA	CASTELLANO/COMP
12:30–1:15	ED. FÍSICA	FÍSICA	QUÍMICA	CAT. BOLIVAR	ED. FÍSICA
1:15–2:00	ED. FÍSICA	BIOLOGÍA	COMPUTAC.	BIOLOGÍA	BIOLOGÍA

Class schedule at Unidad Educativa Academia Washington. "Horario de clase, grado 9no." Reprinted by permission of *Unidad Educativa Academia Washington.*

REALIA

Realia 3-2

TELEAGENDA

hora	6	TELEAMAZONAS	TELESISTEMA	ECUAVISA	TELEVISIÓN	13	TELE ANDINA 23	VeintiCinco XX5
6:00 / 6:30	Buenos días agricultor	Despertares Esta mañana	Noticiero Telem.	NBC News	Dibujos Club 700	Buenos días Euronews		Noticias
7:00 / 7:30	Primera hora Protagonistas	Deporte total	La noticia Copa	Contacto directo	Noti 10	Aprendiendo a vivir Noticiero		Menú de Karlos A Lingo
8:00 / 8:30	Mucho gusto	Vanidades Teve	Club telemundo	Tiro libre Complicidades	Acción de Noti 10 D'Cocina	Telediario Telenegocios		TV educativa
9:00 / 9:30	Para usted Dibujos	Toque de Mariaca Cine: A veces se	Animados	Gino Mollinari	El mundo infantil de TC	Directo Tve TV mandato		Telediario-1 TV Educativa
10:00 / 10:30	Clásicos del cine mexicano	dice una mentira		Princesa		Euronews TV mandato		Vuelta ciclística a
11:00 / 11:30		La traidora	Cara a cara: Me visto como me	Por estas calles	TC cine: Idilio pre- sente	Mundo de cada día Primera respuesta		España
12:00 / 12:30	Gasparín Protagonistas	Deporte total	da la gana Primer impacto	Telebreves Bonanza		Lingo		Noticias Los Fruitis
13:00 / 13:30	Polivoces Medio día	24 horas	El Pirrurris Aló que tal	Televistazo Video Show	Noti 10 Sintonizando	Telenegocios Deutsche Welle		
14:00 / 14:30	En familia con Mercedes	Aquí Mariela Marielena		Cuando llega el	Geraldo: Los	Tventas Aventura del saber	Big Bam Boom	Menú de Karlos A
15:00 / 15:30	Alcanzar una estrella	Inés Duarte	Ocurrió así	amor Señora	dobles de los famosos		Safari	Telediario 2 Aventuras el saber
16:00 / 16:30	Deportes espec- taculares	Club de Disney	Cristina	Liveman	El engaño	Sinvergüenza Deutsche welle	Tertulias (r)	
17:00 / 17:30		Supercampeones Carrusel	Feria de la ale- gría	Yo amo a Lucy Chapulín	Potra Zaina	TV mandato	Secretos de familia	Primera respuesta
18:00 / 18:30	Enamorada Noticiero	Pícara soñadora		Antonella	Morena Clara	Informativo USIS Menú de Karlos A	Mundo de hoy Big Bam Boom	Aventura del saber
19:00 / 19:30	Más allá del hori- zonte	Pasionaria	Servicio secreto	Dejate querer	Sirena	Tventas Deutsche welle	Edición 23	Primera respuesta
20:00 / 20:30	Noticiero Más allá del	24 horas Dos mujeres y un	Corazón salvaje	Televistazo En cuerpo y	Noti 10	Informativo USIS Telediario	Noticiero D.	Fútbol Vefa Pasa la vida
21:00 / 21:30	puente Comedias	camino Aventura del cine:	Tres destinos	alma Hombres	Despedida de soltero	Senderos isleños ¿Quién sabe dónde?	Los Bertini	
22:00 / 22:30	Noticiero	Atrapado sin sali- da	La noticia Copa	duros: "El duro"	Cine de estre- llas: Donato y		Grandes obras maestras	Resumen vuelta
23:00 / 23:30	Basquetbol de la NBA	Media noche	Ocurrió así	Cine club	Diana Mundo de hoy	Noticias	Secretos de familia	ciclística
24:00 / 24:30		Aquí Mariela (r) Cierre			Geraldo (r)	Primera respuesta	Worldnet	¿Quién sabe dónde? Telediario 2
1:00 / 1:30						Wornet		Resumen vuelta ciclística a España
2:00 / 2:30						Austin City		Euronews Telediario matinal
3:00 / 3:30								Desayunos de radio
4:00 / 4:30						Directo Tve		Aventuras del saber
5:00 / 5:30								Primera respuesta

"Teleagenda" from *Hoy*, Tuesday, May 3, 1994. Copyright © 1994 by *Editores e Impresores, S.A.* Reprinted by permission of the publisher.

Cumpleaños feliz

El Centenario del Cine fue celebrado con un amplio número de films, muy variado en cuanto a argumentos y estilos.

Desde el otro lado del globo terráqueo, Australia, llegó un film en el que los animales no sólo eran los absolutos protagonistas, sino que también hablaban: *Babe, el cerdito valiente*, relato de un porcino que intenta integrarse como un miembro más en una granja de animales. Mucha gente se divirtió con este peculiar largometraje, pero otros directores se tomaron el término cerdo de forma mucho más seria.

QUE EN *BABE, EL CERDITO VALIENTE*, los animales protagonistas pudieron hablar dependió de la cuidada labor de las técnicas de animación por ordenador.

MEL GIBSON HIZO un enorme esfuerzo para sacar adelante *Braveheart*, película por la que recibiría los mayores elogios de toda su carrera, especialmente por lo que concernía a sus cualidades como director.

TOY STORY (JUGUETES) arrancaba con una canción, *You've Got a Friend in Me*, creada e interpretada por la inconfundible y quebrada voz del gran Randy Newman. La técnica de animación por ordenador hizo de *Toy Story (Juguetes)* el primer largometraje integramente realizado con ese sistema, en un año en el que la comedia estuvo dignamente representada por *Boca a boca* y por *Two Much*, primera aventura americana de Fernando Trueba, tras el Oscar de *Belle Epoque*. El centenario de cine resultó bastante completo.

Adapted from "1995 Cumpleaños feliz" from *Suplemento Fotogramas No. 1 Libro de oro 50 años de cine* from *Fotogramas & Video*, año L, no. 1.843, May 1997. Copyright © 1997 by **Comunicación y Publicación**. Reprinted by permission of the publisher.

Realia 3-1: Venezuelan High School Schedule

1. **Reading:** First, have students think about what information is usually on a student's school schedule (time, days, classes). Then, have them read the schedule, paying special attention to new vocabulary and cognates.

2. **Listening:** Model the pronunciation of the course (**física, inglés, matemática, química, castellano [castell.], educación física [ed. física], geografía venezolana [geograf. venezla]**) having students repeat after you. For example, **¿Qué tiene el estudiante el lunes a las siete y media?** (**física**) Then ask them some true or false questions. **¿Tiene biología el jueves a las nueve?** (**No**)

3. **Writing:** Divide the class into small groups. Have each group work together to write a daily class schedule for a typical week at your school, including morning and afternoon classes. Then, have two groups trade schedules and discuss differences between their groups' class schedules.

4. **Group work/Speaking:** Have students practice asking each other what classes they have at certain hours on different days, the number of classes they are taking, and the frequency of their classes. Encourage them to use the vocabulary they've learned in Chapter 3.

5. **Culture:** Education in Venezuela is mandatory through sixth grade, which marks the end of elementary school or **primaria**. The majority of students continue in school for secondary education, which lasts for five years. This is called **bachillerato**. After the first three years of high school, students are required to choose a concentration in humanities or sciences. Their classes then intensively prepare them for a specific career direction. All students in Venezuela within a certain concentration are required to take the same classes, and must pass a standardized exam every year. If they fail this exam they will have the opportunity to take it again.

Realia 3-2: Television Guide

1. **Listening/Speaking:** Read aloud the time and the channel of specific programs and have students identify the programs.

2. **Reading:** Have students find two or three of each of the following types of programs and tell at what times they're shown:
   news programs   sporting events   children's programming   movies

3. **Writing:** Have students choose one news program, one sports event, and one children's program and write out the times at which they are shown.

4. **Pair work/Writing/Speaking:** Have students make a list of three or four programs that interest them. Have them exchange their lists with a partner and ask one another the times of the programs.

5. **Culture:** Many TV programs in the Spanish-speaking countries are filmed in front of a live audience in the studio. Some examples of this type of show are: **Programas infantiles** *(children's shows)*, **Programas de variedades al mediodía** *(midday shows)* and **Programas de diálogo** *(talk shows)*. Ask students to make a list of the programs from the television guide, and mention some of their equivalents in the U.S.

Realia 3-3: Movie Review Article

1. **Reading:** Ask students to spend a couple of minutes thinking about what they know about movie reviews. What kind of information is usually included? Then have them quickly skim the article looking for words they recognize. Tell them to consider context as a clue to help them understand unfamiliar words and phrases.

2. **Speaking:** Ask students if they've seen these movies. Ask for volunteers to say if they liked or disliked one of these films in particular or another popular film, and the actors listed. Have students use adjectives they learned in this chapter to describe the movies.

3. **Group work/Writing:** Divide the class into groups of three or four. Have them use the Spanish they know to write a short paragraph describing a film they saw recently. Ask them to select a spokesperson to read their film review to the class.

4. **Culture:** You might point out that Latin American literature has been the inspiration for many movies. There are many famous Latin-American authors whose books have been made into films. The script for "*The Old Gringo* " (**Gringo Viejo**) was based on a novel by the Mexican author Carlos Fuentes; "*The North*" (**El Norte**) came from a novel by the Nicaraguan author Arturo Arias; and "*The House of the Spirits*" (**La Casa de los Espíritus**) is the film version of a novel by the Chilean author Isabel Allende.

REALIA

Realia 4-1

◆ TEATRO ◆ SALAS ◆

CENTRO CULTURAL DE LA VILLA. Plaza de Colón. 575 60 80. Colón y Serrano. Servicio de Telentradas, Caja de Cataluña, 902 38 33 33. Cerrado lunes. **Las aventuras de Don Quijote.** Con la Compañía El Retablo. Pases: Dom. 16.45 h. **Ciclo de las Estrellas.** Pases: Ver sección «Música»

CIRCULO DE BELLAS ARTES. Marqués de Casa Riera, 2 (Esquina con Alcalá. 531 77 00. **El visitante.** De: Eric-Emmanuel Schmitt. Director: Ángel García Moreno. Con Manuel Galiana,

Luis Merlo, Ana Labordeta y Jesús Ruyman. Pases: Martes, miércoles y jueves, 19.30 h. Viernes y sábados, 19.30 y 22.45 h. Domingos, 17 y 19.30 h.

INFANTA ISABEL. Barquillo, 24. 521 47 78. Banco y Colón. Aparcamiento Plaza del Rey y Augusto Figueroa Telentradas en el 902 38 33 33. **¿Qué fue de las hermanas Sue?.** Director: Manu Berástegi. Con Las Veneno. Pases: Martes, miércoles, jueves y domingo, a las 20 h. Vier. y sáb. 19.30 y 22.30 h. Lunes, descanso. **Por**

delante y... por detrás. De: Michael Frayn. Pases: Miércoles, 19.30 h. Jueves, viernes y sábados, 19 y 22.30 h. Domingos, 19 h. Lunes y martes, descanso.

MARAVILLAS. Manuela Malasaña, 6. 446 71 94. Bilbao. Miércoles, día del espectádor. Domingos primera función, precios reducidos. Precios especiales para grupos. Venta anticipada en taquilla, de 11.30 a 13.30 y de 17.30 a 23 h. Reservas en el 446 71 94. Servicio de teleentradas 538 33 33. Lunes, descanso.

◆ MÚSICA ◆ CONCIERTOS ◆

OTRAS MÚSICAS

Lo'Jo. Lirismo étnico, en la sala **Caracol** (Bernardino Obregón, 18), a las 22.00 h. 1.000 pts.

Jorge Pardo & Malik Yaqub Cuarteto. Jazz. En el **Café Jazz Populart** (Huertas, 22), a las 23.00 y 02.00 h. Suplemento actuación, 250 pts.

David Mengual. Jazz homenajeando al gran Thelonious Monk, el **Café Central** (Plaza del Ángel, 10), a las 22.00 h. 800 pts.

Said Ooghassal. Melodías de Marruecos. En **La Boca del Lobo** (Echegaray, 11), a las 24.00 h. Entrada libre.

INTENSAS GUITARRAS DESDE SAN FRANCISCO

En 1989 ropieron los esquemas de San Francisco con su primer disco. Hace poco, Swell lo ha vuelto a hacer con el guitarrero *Too many days without thinking*. Lo presentan en Madrid, el domingo 4 en Moby Dick a las 22.40 h. 600 pts.

Stage Hair Show. Raro. En el **Galileo Galilei** (Galileo, 100), a las 22.00 h. Entrada libre.

MARTES, 6 DE MAYO

POP-ROCK

Randy Slits. Rock and roll. En el **Tupper-ware** (Corredera Alta

de San Pablo, 26), a las 23.00 h. Entrada libre.

Eduarto Martí. Country, en el **Rincón del Arte Nuevo** (Segovia, 17), a las 23.30 h. Entrada libre.

NOCHE DE REYES

Ya es de noche en este pequeño pueblo pero todavía hay gente en la calle. Los Reyes quieren dejar su regalo en la casa de Gabriel. Pero... *1-* ¿Podrías decir cuál es la casa de Gabriel, sabiendo que tiene tres ventanas, techo de tejas, dos columnas en la puerta y una enredadera en el frente?; *2-* ¿Qué camino deben tomar los Reyes para llegar a la casa de Gabriel sin cruzarse con nadie?; *3-* Por la calle hay dos personas exactamente iguales. ¿Cuáles son?; *4-* Todos los círculos contienen una parte de esta escena, menos uno. ¿Cuál?

SOLUCIÓN: *1-* Es la de abajo, a la derecha.; *2-* Entran por la diagonal, giran a la izquierda, dan vuelta a la manzana de la iglesia, cruzan el puente de escaleras, pasan por detrás de los árboles, pasan bajo el arco y siguen hacia la derecha hasta la casa.; *3-* Los dos barrenderos.; *4-* El número 4.

Realia 4-3

nósotros

Ganas de triunfar

Pedro llegará a ser una estrella de rock

Pedro tiene una sonrisa tímida y unas manos enormes que cuando tocan la guitarra se transforman. Aún no sabe qué estilo musical prefiere. De momento, le gusta tocar rock, flamenco y melodías. Quiere componer sus propias canciones por eso estudia solfeo. Sus héroes son Bruce Springsteen y Paco de Lucía. Además de la música le encanta el fútbol. Estas dos aficiones no tienen nada en común pero dice que eso no importa.

Elena sueña con ser una gran bailaora

Elena No pertenece a una familia de artistas pero parece que creció con unos zapatos de tacón en los pies. Le gustaría no hacer otra cosa, sólo bailar. Sus padres piensan que debe estudiar. Ella es joven pero no le falta energía ni talento para llegar a ser una estupenda bailaora. Su sueño es tener algún día su propia compañía de flamenco y viajar por el mundo.

¿Y tú? ¿Qué quieres llegar a ser?

Text and photos from "Nósotros Ganas de Triunfar" from *Ahora*, vol. 1, no. 4, March 1995. Copyright © 1995 by *Scholastic Inc.* Reprinted by permission of the publisher.

REALIA

Realia 4-1: Cultural events guide

1. **Reading:** Have students read over the cultural events guide. What do they think is the meaning of the words **precio** (*price*) and **aparcamiento**? (*parking*)

2. **Listening:** Ask students to tell you the times of various performances and other pieces of information from the article. Which performances listed would they like to attend?

3. **Speaking:** Divide the class into seven groups and assign each group a day of the week. Have them discuss what they would do during that day to have fun if they had to choose events from the guide.

4. **Writing/Group work:** Divide the students into small groups. Have the students write a list describing the activities from the guide that are the most popular among their peers. Which days of the week do students more frequently have fun? Which day is the busiest for students?

5. **Speaking:** Have a spokesperson from each group report to the class what their group chose as the most popular activities.

6. **Culture:** In many Spanish-speaking countries students receive a special rate when they use their ID cards to buy tickets for movies, plays, and concerts. Many plays and art exhibitions are **entrada libre** (*free of charge*) during certain days and times of the week.

Realia 4-2: Three Kings Night

1. **Speaking:** Use expressions of location from Chapter 4 **Vocabulario** to demonstrate how to tell and to ask where objects and people are in the classroom. Have students work with a partner asking and telling each other where people and objects are in the room.

2. **Reading:** Have students pair up and read **Noche de Reyes** in order to identify buildings, animals and people in the reading. Ask them to use expressions of location to demonstrate on the map the answers given in the **solución**.

3. **Writing/Speaking:** Divide the class into groups of three or four. Have each group draw a map of their city, school or neighborhood. Students should use points of reference in order to practice asking and answering questions about the location of people and things on their maps. Ask spokespersons from each group to present to the class.

4. **Culture:** Explain to students that in Spanish-speaking countries it is a tradition to give Christmas gifts on the sixth of January. This Catholic tradition celebrates the visit of the Three Kings to the newborn Jesus. On January fifth, each child prepares a box with fresh-cut grass, flowers, or dried corn. They put the box under their beds or in the living room and wait for the next day. When they wake up on January 6, the camels (or horses) will have eaten the grass, and the Three Kings will have left gifts for the children.

Realia 4-3: Interviews

1. **Reading:** Have students scan the article for cognates, new vocabulary, and familiar names. Ask students to supply at least four facts about Elena and Pedro.

2. **Speaking:** Have students work with a partner and ask each other: Where do they go during their free time? What do they do for fun?

3. **Writing:** Ask each group to write a short dialogue about the activites they do in their free time, and where they go to have fun.

4. **Group work/Speaking:** Have students work in groups of four. Students should take turns interviewing the other members of the group asking questions from the dialogue and take notes on their answers. You may want to call one person at random to report to the class the most popular activity and place to go during their spare time.

5. **Culture:** You might point out that Andalusia is the home of **flamenco** (a dance that incorporates guitar music, finger-snapping, castanets, and heel-stomping). Ask how many in the class have heard **flamenco** music or have seen **flamenco** dancing. If possible, you may wish to play a portion of a **flamenco** tape or video.

REALIA

Los alimentos

Démosle un vistazo a la comida que te ayuda a crecer fuerte, sano y contento.

El **desayuno** es importante. Un *vaso de leche*, una *tostada* y un *jugo de frutas* es lo ideal. ¿No te gusta la leche? Prepárate un *licuado*, así juntás la leche y la fruta. No tomés cacao todos los días, éste impide que el calcio de la leche se absorba. ¿Si desayunás se te hace tarde? Y... levantate más temprano.

Los panchos y las hamburguesas gigantes son ricos, pero si éste es tu **almuerzo** de todos los días ¡hummm!, no vas a estar bien alimentado. Una *buena porción de carne*, una *ensalada* y para el postre una *fruta*, te aseguran un almuerzo nutritivo y sano. Probá... ¡Vas a ver cómo te gusta!

¡A tomar la leche! Llegó la hora de la **merienda**. Si te gusta el *yogur* ésta es tu oportunidad. Podés mezclarlo *con copos*, *con frutas* o *con pedacitos de galletitas*. Claro que podés comer una porción de torta de chocolate, de ésa que hizo la abuela. Pero una porción... ¡no una torta *entera*!

Después del baño... **¡a cenar!** ¿Sabías que *las pastas* son un buen alimento? ¿Quién se niega a comer un plato de *fideos*, *ñoquis* o *ravioles con salsa de tomate*? Si los probaste con salsa y no te gustaron, podés condimentar tus pastas con un poco de manteca, aceite o salsa blanca.

Text and art from "Los alimentos" from "Ciencias naturales" section from *Billiken*, no. 4034, May 2, 1997. Copyright © 1997 by *Editorial Atlántida, S.A.* Reprinted by permission of the publisher.

◆ **Realia 5-2**

CALENDARIO DEPORTIVO

Deporte: EL SQUASH
Campeonato: el Open Mundial
Lugar: Barcelona, España
Fecha: del 2 al 11 de septiembre

El squash es bastante popular en España ahora. Incluso el rey Juan Carlos lo practica.

octubre

L	M	M	J	V	S	D
					1	2
3	4	5	6	7	8	9
10	11	12	13	14	15	16
17	18	19	20	21	22	23
24	25	26	27	28	29	30
31						

Deporte: EL WINDSURF
Carrera: campeonato de Europa
Lugar: La Manga, España
Fecha: del 1 al 8 de octubre

El windsurf, a nivel internacional, es un deporte muy emocionante y España tiene lugares estupendos para practicarlo como Tarifa en el sur de España y Lanzarote en las Islas Canarias.

septiembre

L	M	M	J	V	S	D
			1	2	3	4
5	6	7	8	9	10	11
12	13	14	15	16	17	18
19	20	21	22	23	24	25
26	27	28	29	30		

Deporte: EL BEISBOL
Campeonato: la Serie Mundial
Lugar: Estados Unidos
Fecha: empieza a mediados de octubre

Hay muchos jugadores de béisbol muy buenos de Latinoamérica que juegan en las Ligas Mayores en Estados Unidos.
El béisbol es muy popular en Cuba, Puerto Rico, la República Dominicana, Colombia, Venezuela y México.

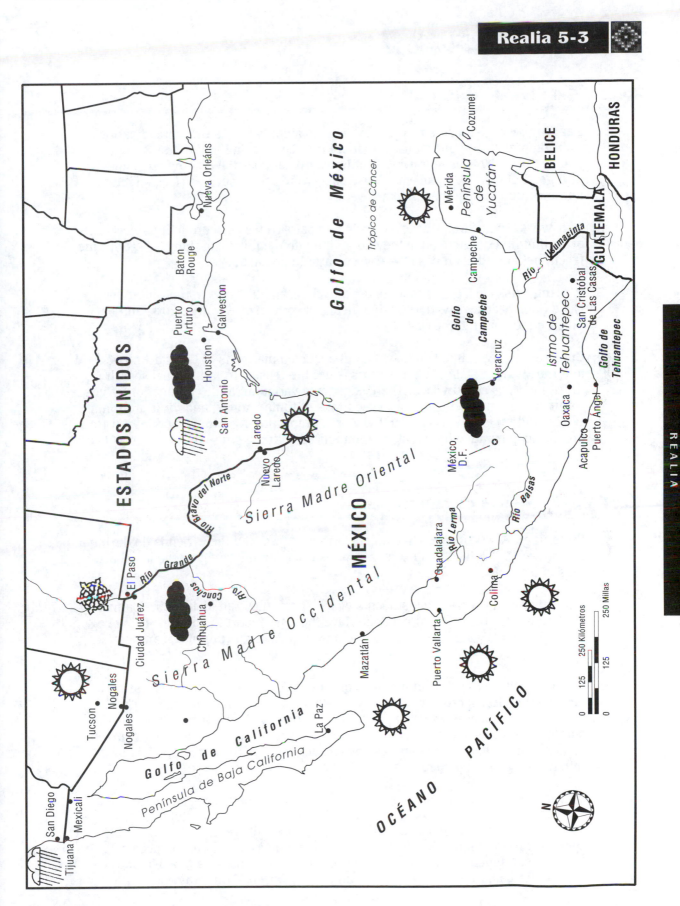

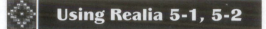
Realia 5-1: Meals cartoon

1. **Reading:** Have students read the captions to identify words they already know. Ask comprehension questions. (What are the people doing in the first, second, and last picture? Which drawing is of lunch? What does the reading recommend as a good dinner? Tell students to use background clues such as clocks, foods, and furniture to help them find answers.

2. **Pair work/Speaking:** Divide the class into pairs. Have each group interview each other and find out how often they do or don't do the following things: —¿**Con qué frecuencia ayudas en casa?** —**A veces ayudo en casa.**

3. **Writing:** Ask each group to write the questions and answers to their interview. Have them peer review their writing, help each other correct any errors, and be prepared to report to the class.

4. **Culture:** In Argentina, Uruguay, Paraguay, Colombia, parts of Central America, and the Mexican state of Chiapas, **vos** is used to replace **tú** in informal speech. This practice is called **voseo**. There is regional variation in the conjugation of **vos** forms. In Argentina the present tense forms of **tomar**, **tener**, and **vivir** are **tomás**, **tenés**, and **vivís**. In this cartoon the words **preparate**, **No tomés**, and **levantate** are in the imperative form and are pronounced with the stress on the next-to-last syllable.

Realia 5-2: Sports calendar

1. **Listening:** Ask students what athletic activities they and their friends do during a typical week. Tell them to look at the sports calendar and compare the listed activities to their own.

2. **Reading/Group work:** Ask students which sports they can identify in Spanish by looking only at the calendar pictures. Have the class report to you how many cognates they find. Write a list of their findings on the board. (**popular, campeonato, estupendos, etc.**)

3. **Writing:** Divide the class into groups of four. Ask students first to discuss and develop the ideal sports program they would like to have in their school. Then, have them consider in which sports they and other students would like to participate. Each group should have a note taker who will write their sports schedule in Spanish on the board. The class as a whole will vote for the schedules that best reflect their general preferences.

4. **Culture:** Schools in Spanish-speaking countries don't have sports programs like schools in the U.S. Students usually participate in private sports clubs or city leagues. For economic reasons, baseball and basketball are the most accessible sports for most young athletes. Baseball can be practiced without the need of a ball or a bat. Ingenious young players might use a broomstick as the bat and pebbles for ball. Roberto Clemente began playing baseball this way.

Realia 5-3: Weather map

1. **Listening/Speaking:** Have students read over the weather map. Ask them to identify a place where the weather is warm, rainy, etc. Then, name a place on the map and ask students to describe the weather there.

2. **Writing:** Have students write a description of the weather for their home city on a typical day in different seasons.

3. **Pair work/Speaking:** Ask students to interview each other about which places on the map they would like to visit and why. The interview should include questions about why they would or would not like to visit based on the kinds of things they like to do. **(En octubre quiero ir a ...; En verano quieres ir a ...)**

4. **Culture:** The Tropic of Cancer cuts through the middle of Mexico and acts as a divider between two general climates: the **tierra caliente** to the south of the Tropic of Cancer and the **tierra fría** to the north. Climate also depends on altitude as well as latitude. The climate in the mountains is cooler than in the low-lying plains below (the **tierra templada**). Have students locate the equator on the map. Point out that seasons in the southern cone of South America occur at the opposite time of year from countries north of the equator. Summer begins in December and winter in June. In the lowlands of South America located on or near the equator, the weather is warm all year round, and there are only two seasons, wet and dry. Throughout the Americas, altitude plays a major role in climate. For example, the Andes are quite cold even though they traverse the equator.

Realia 6-1

MUNDO JOVEN...

MATI, NUESTRA LECTORA DEL MES HABLA DE SU FAMILIA: "SOMOS SUPER DIFERENTES PERO MUY UNIDOS..."

Mati hall, una lectora de tampa, es la ganadora del concurso "la familia más original". di tú si no tenemos razón:

"Tengo un hermano que quiero mucho, Jonathan. Jonathan es dos meses mayor que yo... ¿qué raro verdad? Bueno, es que los dos somos adoptados. Mis padres, Mark y Guadalupe Hall—mi mamá es mexicana—decidieron adoptar en lugar de tener hijos propios. A mi papá le gusta que la gente le pregunte por qué todos somos tan diferentes. Siempre tiene una respuesta original porque es muy gracioso. Cuando salimos a restaurantes o a lugares públicos la gente siempre nos mira, imagínense, yo soy asiática, Jonathan afro-americano, mi mamá de México y mi padre norteamericano de pelo rubio. ¡Somos una ensalada! Bueno, les mando una foto mía y de Jonathan, ojalá que ganemos el concurso, tengo muchas ganas de conocer México y practicar mi español. Lo escribo bien, ¿no?

¡LO ESCRIBES EXCEPCIONAL, MATI! Y CLARO, TÚ Y TU FAMILIA ESTARÁN MUY PRONTO VISITÁNDONOS EN EL D.F. ¡CHAO!

REALIA

Cómo brillan nuestros deportistas hispanos

Pablo Morales

Mary Joe Fernández

Alto, delgado y de gran fuerza espiritual, lo más impresionante de este atleta hispano es su capacidad para salir de los momentos difíciles. En los Juegos Olímpicos de 1992 Pablo dedicó su medalla de oro a la memoria de su madre, Blanca, quien murió de cáncer. Aunque ella no estaba allí, Pablo sabía que ella estaba contenta. Hoy, el gran nadador es un empresario de éxito en la industria de los productos acuáticos.

Esta deportista, hija de madre cubana y padre español, ha ganado dos medallas de oro consecutivas en dobles de tenis en las Olimpiadas de 1992 y 1996. Mary Joe es considerada una de las mejores tenistas de hoy. Aunque es delgada tiene brazos fuertes. Es joven y ha ganado torneos en todo el mundo.

LIMPIEZA DE LA CASA

Nuestra compañía profesional con 15 años de experiencia ofrece servicios de limpieza de casa: planchar, hacer las camas, limpiar la cocina, los baños, la sala y los cuartos. Podemos transformar su hogar y hacer más cómodo el estar en casa.

¡Empiece ahora!

También ofrecemos servicios de jardín y de animales: cortar el césped, recoger las hojas y cuidar al gato.
Teléfono 334-23-04. Los Condes

Realia 6-1 : Mundo Joven contest

1. **Listening:** Use Teaching Transparency 6–1 to introduce the concept of a family tree. Ask students comprehension questions based on this visual.

2. **Reading:** Have students read over the article. Remind them to look for cognates and known vocabulary. Ask them to identify a characteristic that describes the family, and what it is that makes the family in the letter so unique.

3. **Writing:** Explain to students that the family in the article won a trip to Mexico City. Ask them to write a letter to the magazine **Mundo Joven** describing their own family. The focus of their letter should be to identify what makes their family unique.

4. **Speaking/Group work:** Divide the class into groups of three or four. Have students share their letters with group members and vote on which is the most original family in their group. Ask the winner of each group to describe their family to the class.

5. **Culture:** In Latin American countries it's normal for three generations to live together in the same house and for everyone to help around the house. **La familia** often includes aunts, uncles, cousins, grandparents, and godparents. If a member of the family becomes disabled, old, or ill and needs special care, the others will take turns taking care of that person. Extended families are committed to take care of their elderly because they are a source of wisdom and experience. Younger generations learn from their parents to respect and look after the elderly members of their family. Nursing homes aren't a preference for the extended family. Since extended families keep close ties, when a couple has a child, everyone participates in bringing up the child. The concept of a family in the Hispanic culture is centered around unity and loyalty to all family members.

Realia 6-2: Sports stars article

1. **Listening:** Before handing out copies of the article, read it aloud. Have students take notes on what they hear you read about Pablo Morales and Mary Joe Fernández. Ask students to list cognates as they listen. Write the list of cognates students report they heard on the board or a transparency. Ask what facts they know about Mary Joe and Pablo. Affirm those which are correct by repeating appropriate phrases from the reading.

2. **Reading:** Hand out copies and have the class read the article, noticing cognates. Have students look at the following words: (**tribunas** *grandstand*, **ahogarse** *to drown*, **falleció** *died*, **nadador** *swimmer*, **empresario** *businessman*, **desarrollarse** *to develop*). Then, ask them to guess the meaning by looking at context.

3. **Writing/Group work:** Divide the class into groups of four. Have each group write a composition about a favorite athlete. Ask one student from each group to represent their group and report on what they wrote, but not to give the name of their favorite athlete. Ask the class to guess the athlete's name.

4. **Culture:** Spanish-speaking athletes have contributed greatly to the world of sports, including baseball, boxing, soccer, tennis and swimming. Fans in Latin American countries have had a lot to cheer about! In 1993 and 1994, Sergi Bruguera of Spain won the French Open, one of the four Grand Slam events in professional tennis. During the Atlanta Olympics of 1996, Bruguera was a finalist in tennis singles. Another Latin American tennis star, Chilean Marcelo Ríos, finished in 1996 number 11 in the world. In 1994, Conchita Martínez became the first Spanish woman to win the Wimbledon crown, tennis's premier tournament. Hispanics are also well represented in swimming. During the 1996 Atlanta Olympics, Cuban swimmers Rodolfo Falcón and Neisser Bent won the silver and bronze medals in the 100 meter back stroke, and Claudia Poll from Costa Rica won the gold medal in the 200 meter freestyle.

Realia 6-3: Housecleaning services ad

1. **Listening:** Before distributing copies to students, read the ad aloud to see if they can guess the topic of the ad.

2. **Listening/Reading:** Call out a specific household chore in Spanish and ask the students if this ad offers that service.

3. **Speaking:** Have students name all the household chores that this ad offers.

4. **Writing:** Have small groups of students cooperatively write a classified ad similar to the one in the realia.

5. **Culture:** In Puerto Rico, Santo Domingo and Cuba, it is a tradition to clean and paint the house before the New Year. Many Caribbeans believe that they will have good luck during the entire new year if their houses are very clean and well painted. Another reason linked to the traditional cleaning of the house is **las parrandas** or **asaltos** celebrated during the Christmas season. Families and groups of friends travel house to house all night, paying surprise visits, singing **villancicos** *(carols)* and playing Christmas music. Every **parranda** becomes an instant party where people dance, sing, and eat all night long.

Mientras Ud. no estaba

Recado telefónico

Para el/la Sr(a).

De parte de

De la compañía	Teléfono

Dijo que

( ) le llamara Ud. al regresar

( ) llamaría más tarde

Recado:

Recibido por	Hora	Fecha

Realia 7-2

Una mascarilla facial es la mejor forma para cuidar tu cutis. Depende del tipo de piel que tú tienes. Puedes usar una mascarilla hidratante (seca) o una exfoliadora (grasosa). Aplícatela mientras te bañas, te afeitas o te peinas tu cabello. Tu piel va a estar suave y radiante.

REALIA

Adapted text and photo from "Viernes 24: ¡La gran noche del año! Un paso a paso completo para brillar en Navidad" from *Tú internacional*, año 14, no. 12, December 1993. Copyright © 1993 by *Editorial Televisa.* Reprinted by permission of the publisher.

¡Ven conmigo! Level 1, Chapter 7

Te invitamos...

¡...porque no sería fiesta sin ti!

VAMOS A FESTEJAR A:

_____

CON MOTIVO DE:

_____

FECHA:

_____

HORA:

_____

DIRECCIÓN:

_____

¡Te esperamos!

Junto con nuestros padres

Sres. Valero-Litri   *Sres. Puig-Roca*

Tenemos el gusto de invitaros a nuestra boda,
que celebraremos el día 10 de mayo próximo,
en la Iglesia Ntra. Sra. de los Ángeles,
a las 6 de la tarde.

Miguel y Montserrat

Cena: Restaurante: La Piel del Oso   *Rogamos confirmación*   *Port Bou, 1999*

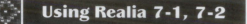

Realia 7-1: Telephone message pad

1. **Reading:** Ask students to identify this piece of realia and to try to infer the meanings of phrases like **dijo que le llamara Ud. al regresar** and **llamaría más tarde.** Ask students to guess the meanings of several words such as **mientras, compañía,** and **recibido por.** Ask them if they can recognize the verb **estaba** as a form of **estar.**

2. **Listening/Writing:** Have students take messages. For example: **favor de llamar al señor Rodríguez lo más antes posible,** or **Julio quiere saber si te gustaría ir al museo este sábado.**

3. **Pair work/Speaking:** Have students create and then act out a business telephone call. For example: one student is a receptionist or secretary and the other is a client trying to reach an executive. The executive will be out and the receptionist will take a message.

4. **Culture:** You might point out to students that in many Spanish-speaking countries they need to buy tokens to use a **teléfono público** *(pay phone)*. There is no time limit on local calls. The tokens are available for purchase in candy stores or newspaper stands. For long distance calls they may need to go to a government telephone company: **ENTEL** in Chile, **Teléfonos de México** in México, **GUATEL** in Guatemala, **IETEL** in Ecuador, and **CANTV** in Venezuela.

Realia 7-2: Facial ad

1. **Reading/Speaking:** Have students read the ad text. Ask students to identify known words and those that are unfamiliar to them. Model a discussion with the students about what the person in the picture needs to do in order to get ready to go out.

2. **Writing:** Have students use known vocabulary to list activities that comprise their daily routines for a week. How long do they take to get ready for each of their daily activities?

3. **Pair work:** Divide the class into pairs. Give each pair one of the following situation: **el lago, una fiesta de cumpleaños, una boda** and **una fiesta de graduación.** Pairs discuss what they need to do and how much time they need to get ready to go out to these locations.

4. **Culture:** The most popular free-time activities among teenagers in Spanish-speaking countries are group activities. Young people like to get together at parks, cafés, private homes, or social clubs. They enjoy listening to music, talking, watching a video, playing sports, or just spending time together. Dressing well is very important for both girls and boys. Everything in their outfit needs to match or be coordinated with their shoes or jewelry. It is also popular to wear good quality fragrances.

Realia 7-3: Social Invitations

1. **Listening:** Before distributing copies to students, read each of the announcements aloud to see if they can guess what the celebration is.

2. **Writing:** Have students write an invitation to a ceremony or celebration of their own. It can be a religious ceremony, a birthday party, or a holiday celebration.

3. **Pair work:** Have pairs of students think of a special occasion and use the invitation they did in activity two above to invite friends and/or family to a celebration. Have them present their invitations to the class.

4. **Speaking:** Have students role-play a situation in which one person invites the other to a birthday or wedding and the other either accepts or declines the invitation.

5. **Culture:** You might point out to students that Hispanic people often ask their friends to go to a **restaurante** or a **café al aire libre** to enjoy the art of conversation. **Te invito** means not only "I'm inviting you," but also "I'd like to pay your way." People follow the Spanish saying: **"Él que invita es él que paga."** *(The one who invites is the one who pays.)*

Realia 8-1

ZUMO EL ANDALUZ
1 lt.
75

CROQUETAS TÍA
ISABEL
500 grs.
175

Pizza Napoli

° PIZZAS NAPOLI
Tamaño mediano
175

POLLO ENTERO, kg.
189

Huevos Categoría Extra
docena, 60/65 grs.
138

MARGARINA
Clavel 500 GRS

Queso Del Campo,
16 lonchas
175

Margarina Clavel
500 grs.
119

FRUTAS Y VERDURAS

Naranjas	Piñas	Plátanos	Peras
110 pts./kg.	**13** pts./kg.	**145** pts./kg.	**95** pts./kg.

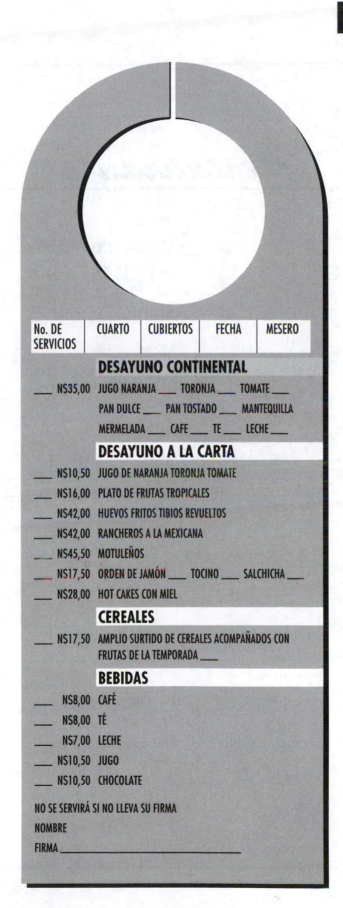

No. DE SERVICIOS	CUARTO	CUBIERTOS	FECHA	MESERO

DESAYUNO CONTINENTAL

____ N$35,00 JUGO NARANJA ____ TORONJA ____ TOMATE ____

PAN DULCE ____ PAN TOSTADO ____ MANTEQUILLA ____

MERMELADA ____ CAFE ____ TE ____ LECHE ____

DESAYUNO A LA CARTA

____ N$10,50 JUGO DE NARANJA TORONJA TOMATE

____ N$16,00 PLATO DE FRUTAS TROPICALES

____ N$42,00 HUEVOS FRITOS TIBIOS REVUELTOS

____ N$42,00 RANCHEROS A LA MEXICANA

____ N$45,50 MOTULEÑOS

____ N$17,50 ORDEN DE JAMÓN ____ TOCINO ____ SALCHICHA ____

____ N$28,00 HOT CAKES CON MIEL

CEREALES

____ N$17,50 AMPLIO SURTIDO DE CEREALES ACOMPAÑADOS CON
FRUTAS DE LA TEMPORADA ____

BEBIDAS

____ N$8,00 CAFÉ

____ N$8,00 TÉ

____ N$7,00 LECHE

____ N$10,50 JUGO

____ N$10,50 CHOCOLATE

NO SE SERVIRÁ SI NO LLEVA SU FIRMA

NOMBRE

FIRMA _____

R
E
A
L
I
A

Realia 8-3

Café Restaurante

APERITIVO

Camarones al Ajillo...............75.00

Salpicón de Mariscos............80.00

ENSALADAS

Ensalada Mixta....................35.00

Ensalada César................50.00 p/p

ASADOS Y CARNES

Brocheta de Filete................80.00

Punta de Filete...................85.00

Filete a la Parrilla................ 80.00

Filete Migñón.....................85.00

Filete a la Pimienta..............85.00

PESCADOS Y MARISCOS

Mero a la Parrilla..................85.00

Mero en Escabeche...............90.00

Mero a la Bretona.................95.00

Mero con Mariscos.............100.00

Mero a la Naranja.................95.00

Langosta a su Estilo................S/M

Chillo Empanado.................110.00

Paella Marinera............125.00 p/p

Paella Valenciana..........125.00 p/p

Mero a la Vasca.....................95.00

Cazuela de Mariscos............110.00

Gambas al Ajillo..................140.00

Camarones al Ajillo..............125.00

Realia 8-1: Supermarket ad

1. **Reading:** Have students look over the ad and then ask them what kind of store is being advertised. Point out the words **zumo, piña,** and the abbreviation **pts.** Then ask students what country they think this ad comes from.

2. **Listening:** Prepare a list of some common foods. Include some of the foods that are in the ad and some that aren't. Read your list aloud and ask students to say whether each item you mention is advertised or not. Name the price of some items and have students identify the item by name.

3. **Writing:** Have students prepare a grocery list based on the ad. Then ask them to write a meal they can prepare with the groceries. Tell students to include three items they might also need that are not in the ad.

4. **Pair work/Speaking:** Have students work in pairs and tell each other what they're going to buy for the meal they've planned. Ask students to report their partner's choices to the class.

5. **Culture:** In many Spanish-speaking countries when people want to buy groceries or other items, they prefer to go to specialty stores. (**panadería/pastelería** *bakery*, **carnicería** *butcher's shop*, **frutería** *fruit shop*, **comisaría** *grocery store*, and **lechería** *dairy produce store*) Ask students to compare these specialty stores with the stores they are familiar with in the U.S.

Realia 8-2: Room service menu

1. **Reading:** Have students read over the menu, and then ask them what meal can be ordered from this menu. Where do they think this menu is from?

2. **Pair work/Reading:** Have students work in pairs. Ask them to use context to guess unfamiliar words and phrases such as **salchicha, mantequilla, mermelada, frutas de la temporada,** and **No se servirá si no lleva su firma.**

3. **Listening:** Imagine that you're ordering over the phone and have students take your order. Ask them to check off the items on the menu.

4. **Pair work/Speaking:** Have students work in pairs and take each other's orders. The student who takes the order should also add up the bill and then tell his or her partner the total.

5. **Group work/Writing:** Have students work in groups to create their own room service menus.

6. **Culture:** Puerto Rico has a network of reasonably priced **paradores.** These state-run country farmhouses, often on old sugar haciendas or coffee plantations, offer the authentic atmosphere of Puerto Rican rural life. Surrounded by tropical fruit groves, guests of the **paradores** are welcome to pick their own fresh fruit for breakfast or a snack. Also, fruit baskets, bread, butter, and jam are always available. Ask students to think of and list places that are the U.S. equivalent of **paradores.**

Using Realia 8-3

Realia 8–3: Café Restaurante Menu

1. **Reading:** Have students read over the menu. Ask them which foods and dishes they recognize. Remind students to consider the context and guess the meaning of cognates, such as **mixta** *mix*, **filete** *fillet*, and **estilo** *style*.

2. **Writing:** Divide the class into groups of three or four. Tell them that they are to role-play a meal at the Café Restaurante in which one is the server and the others are customers. The total bill cannot exceed 1,000 **pesos**. Ask them to write and practice performing the skit using Chapter 8 vocabulary and this menu to order and pay for their meal. They must be sure that the 1,000 pesos is enough to cover the price of all of their food, drinks, and tip.

3. **Group work/Speaking:** Have each group present its skit before the class or to circles of two or more groups. Ask follow-up questions: Which customers ordered the most for their 1,000 pesos? Which server and customer were the most patient? The most polite? Which customers gave the best tips? You may wish to videotape the skits.

4. **Culture:** In Spanish-speaking countries, one can find small neigborhood restaurants called **fondas**. These restaurants serve an inexpensive lunch menu, which consists of two or three complete meals from which substitutions cannot be made (**comidas corrientes**). These **fondas** are very popular because cafeterias are rare and fast-food restaurants are generally more expensive than in the U. S. for most people.

ENVUELVE UNA SORPRESA NAVIDEÑA POR MENOS

10⁹⁹
CARTERAS DE MANO PARA DAMAS
Incluye calculadora con teclas de colores. En caja para regalar.

9⁹⁹ Jgo.
ESTUCHES CON CARTERA PARA CABALLEROS Estuche English Leather con cartera y colonia.

13⁹⁹
CARTERAS AMITY PARA CABALLEROS Diferentes estilos.
Otros estilos. 9.99-16.99

Toda la mercancía en esta página está anunciada a nuestro bajo precio regular

4⁹⁹ Caja
PAÑUELOS PARA DAMAS
3 pañuelas de algodón con coloridos bordados. En caja para regalar.

9⁹⁹ Caja
WALLETS 5-EN-1 EN CAJA
Porta tarjeta de crédito, porta chequera, monedero y llavero.

7⁹⁹ Hasta **11⁹⁹**
CARTERAS DE NOCHE
Mini carteras en estilos metálicos.
Correas en lentejelas para damas . . 4.99

4⁹⁹
JOYERIA EN CAJA PARA REGALO
Pendientes, medallones o broches.
Otros jgos. de joyería 9.99
Más 5% de impuestos - Estilos pueden variar entre tiendas.

3⁹⁹
NOVEDOSA JOYERIA* Escoja entre brillantes motivos navideños.
Accesorios para el cabello . . 1.99-2.99
*Más 5% de impuestos - Estilos pueden variar entre tiendas.

5⁹⁹
BUFANDAS NAVIDEÑAS PARA DAMAS Bufandas oblongas con bellos patrones y estampados.
Accesorios para el cabello. . 3.99-4.99
Estilos pueden variar.

Advertisement for K-Mart, "Envuelve una sorpresa Navideña por menos." Reprinted by permission of *K-Mart, Puerto Rico.*

Realia 9-2

Conjuntos formales desde $47.900

Blazer liviano desde $55.200

Pantalones desde $17.600

Fieldjacket desde $47.900

Suéteres desde $12.000

Camisas sport desde $8.900

Pantalones en drill desde $9.900

Medellín: Detrás de la fábrica Everfit-Indulana
              Tel: 2578440

Bogotá: Centro Comercial Niza
              Av. Suba, calle 127.
              Tel: 2533924
              Restrepo
              Calle 18 Sur No. 18-31
              Tel: 3615447

Jean dama desde $15.750

ALMACEN everfit DE FABRICAS

EL PUNTO DE la Calidad

"everfit Almacén de fábricas: El Punto de Calida." Reprinted by permission of *everfit Almacén de fábricas*.

Casa de Modas Primor

Calle Robles, Esq. Ferrocarril Núm. 1200
Río Piedras, Puerto Rico
Tel: (787) 767-4049

NOTA DE REMISIÓN

Fecha : **14 de junio**

No. **235**

Vendedor : **E. Geraldo**

CAN	CONCEPTO	PRECIO	IMPORTE
2	bluejeans	20 x 2	$ 40.00
1	blusa amarilla	50 x 1	$ 50.00
1	cinturón de piel	15 x 1	$ 15.00
2	trajes de seda roja	80 x 2	$ 160,00
	SUBTOTAL		
	IMPUESTO		incluido
		TOTAL	$ 265.00

No se aceptan devoluciones.

REALIA

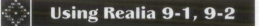

Realia 9-1: Christmas gift catalog

1. **Reading:** Tell students that the prices are in U. S. dollars and ask them where they think this ad might be from. (Puerto Rico) Ask students what words identify the gifts as men's or women's gifts.

2. **Reading:** Ask students to read over the catalog page and make a list of cognates, familiar Spanish words, and any English words that they find. Next ask them to use context to determine unknown words such as **caja**, **bufanda**, etc.

3. **Writing:** Have students make a shopping list of gifts they would like to buy for their family and friends. They may take some or all of their ideas from the catalog page.

4. **Pair work/Speaking:** Divide the class into small groups. Students use the catalog page and their lists and ask one another what gift they want to give the different people on their lists.

5. **Culture:** In many cities in Latin America, locals and tourists can often find the best buys in an open-air market where **el regateo** *(bargaining)* is still customary. At grocery stores or in stores with fixed prices **el regateo** is not permitted. People find it very exciting and interesting to spend time in **la feria de artesanía** *(craft fair)*, **los tianguis la feria** and **el mercadillo** *(open-air markets)*, **el mercado de pulgas** *(flea market)*, where local merchants and artisans exhibit and sell their goods. Ask students if they know places in U.S. where they can **regatear** *(bargain)*.

Realia 9-2: Clothing ad

1. **Listening:** Tell students that this advertisement is from Colombia and that the prices are in Colombian **pesos**. Read some prices and ask students to identify the items by their prices.

2. **Listening:** Ask students which of the items on the page they would wear in the following situations:
   > Hace frío, creo que va a nevar.
   > Tengo una entrevista para trabajar en una oficina.
   > Voy a una fiesta a las ocho.

3. **Pair work/Writing/Speaking:** Ask students to choose a person in the ad and write a detailed description of what that person is wearing. Encourage students to include color, pattern, and whether the item is expensive or inexpensive. Then ask them to work with a partner and have their partner guess who they've just described.

4. **Pair work/Speaking:** Tell students to imagine that this is a page from a catalog and have them work with a partner to place an order over the phone. The customers explain that they like a particular item but want to know if it's available in different colors or patterns. The salesperson responds and then they finalize the sale.

5. **Culture:** The word for **bluejeans** varies by country. People say **mahones** in Puerto Rico, **pantalones vaqueros** in Spain, and **tejanos**, or **pantalones de mezclilla** in México. Other words for **suéter** are **jersey** (Spain), **buzo** (Uruguay), and **chompa** (Perú and Ecuador).The numbers used to indicate clothing sizes in Spain and Latin America are different from those used in the U.S. For example, a women's size 10 in the United States corresponds to a size 42 in Europe and Latin America, and a U.S. men's size 32 in pants is equivalent to a size 81 in Europe.

Realia 9-3: Sales receipt

1. **Reading:** Have students read over the sales receipt. Put the following questions on the board or transparency and allow 1–2 minutes for students to find the answers:
   • What is the name of this store?
   • What kind of store is it? How do you know?
   • How many items were bought, and what kind of things were bought?
   Test students' ability to read for detail and guess from context by asking them to figure out the meaning of the following: **Can.** *(quantity)*, **importe** *(total cost)*, **vendedor** *(salesperson)*, **concepto** *(merchandise)*, and **No se aceptan devoluciones** *(no returns)*.

2. **Writing:** Have students prepare labels for the clothing they are wearing, or for items in their backpacks or gym bags. Each label should identify the item, give a short description, and include the price. For example: **suéter de algodón. Grande y muy cómodo. Precio: $25.00.**

3. **Speaking/Pair work:** Divide students into pairs. Allow 2–3 minutes for one partner to sell his or her labeled items to the other partner, then have pairs reverse roles. Encourage students to incorporate expressions from the **Tercer paso** in their conversation.

4. **Culture:** Have students look at the sales receipt again, this time focusing on the store's address. Ask them if they notice anything ususual about the way that the address is written. Remind students that in Spanish-speaking countries, the building number is usually given after the street name. When a building is located on a corner (**esq.**), often both intersecting street names are included. Have students practice writing their own addresses using this format and filling in the blank portion of the sales receipt.

Realia 10-1

¡Feliz Día de
San Valentín!

Ojalá que no hayas
esperado mucho
mi llamada. . .

¡Feliz Día del Padre!

Quisiera tener todos los
bolívares del mundo para
comprarte un regalo, pero
sólo puedo dártelos en
foto. . . ¡Te quiero
mucho, papá!

RECETA DE TACOS Y BURRITOS MEXICANOS

Estos dos platos mexicanos se hacen con tortillas de maíz. Son muy fáciles de preparar. Aprende la receta y vas a ver qué éxito tienes en tu próxima fiesta.

Burritos con queso
Tortillas de maíz
jamón cocido
queso para gratinar

1. Corta el jamón en tiras.
2. Rellena las tortillas con jamón y queso.
3. Dóblalas por la mitad y caliéntalas un poco en el horno o microondas.
4. Sírvelas en un plato con lechuga y salsa picante.

Tacos vegetarianos
Tortillas de maíz
aguacate
lechuga
limón
pimiento rojo

1. Corta los aguacates y el pimiento rojo en trozos pequeños.
2. Pica la lechuga muy fina.
3. Remuévelo todo bien y pon el jugo de un limón.
4. Rellena las tortillas y enróllalas en forma de tubo.
5. Pon un poco de salsa de chile dentro del taco y vas a ver qué sabrosos.

Salsa picante
Ingredientes para la salsa picante:
tomates picados
sal
cebolla
cilantro
limón
chile picante
aceite

1. Corta los tomates y la cebolla muy pequeños.
2. Mezcla el jugo de un limón con el cilantro y una cucharada de aceite de oliva.
3. Remueve bien todo y añade chile a tu gusto. ¡Cuidado que es muy picante!

Realia 10-3

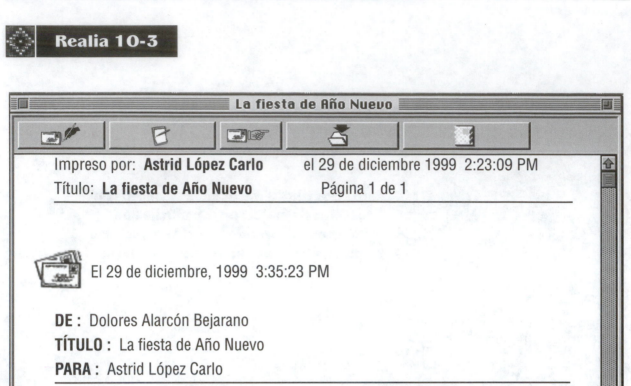

La fiesta de Año Nuevo

Impreso por: **Astrid López Carlo**   el 29 de diciembre 1999 2:23:09 PM
Título: **La fiesta de Año Nuevo**   Página 1 de 1

El 29 de diciembre, 1999 3:35:23 PM

DE : Dolores Alarcón Bejarano
TÍTULO : La fiesta de Año Nuevo
PARA : Astrid López Carlo

Astrid,

El año pasado tuvimos una fiesta sensacional con tu familia y la mía en tu casa. Mi madre me pidió que te recuerde que esta Nochevieja ustedes la van a pasar con nosotros. Ya sé que hablamos de esto el otro día, pero te mando esta carta electrónica por si las dudas. No sé cómo mi mamá va a organizar un evento tan divertido como el que organizó tu mamá. Recuerdo que cantamos, bailamos y comimos mucho. Ayer mi padre me preguntó por tu tío José. ¿Va a venir? Papá quiere que lo invites. Creo que lo conoció en una posada el sábado por la noche. ¿Qué hiciste tú el fin de semana pasado? No te vi en la posada de Guadalupe. Contéstame pronto.

Tu amiga,

Dolores

Realia 10-1: Greeting cards

1. **Reading:** Have students read the text on the greeting cards. Point out that the card reflects a humorus way of looking at a holiday.

2. **Pair work/Speaking:** Have pairs of students discuss gifts for a classmate they both know. Have them use expressions like: **¿Qué te parece si...? Perfecto, Me parece bien, Buena idea, Creo que sí.**

3. **Writing:** Have students design their own greeting card for a friend or family member. It can be a Mother's Day or Father's Day card, or a card for any other holiday.

4. **Culture:** Since extended families keep close ties, Father's Day and Mother's Day are very important in Spanish-speaking countries. Typically, families celebrate and honor their parents, grandparents and the other elderly relatives who share the same home. They celebrate special holidays by going to an early mass, and then returning home for food, music, and gifts.

Realia 10-2: Recipes

1. **Reading:** Have students read the recipes and make a list of familiar words and cognates. List unfamiliar yet important words in the recipes on the board and have students define them as best they can.

2. **Listening:** You might want to practice command forms by writing the following verbs from the recipes on the board or on a transparency: **corta** *(chop or dice)*, **rellena** *(fill or stuff)*, **dóblalas** *(fold them)*, **caliéntalas** *(warm them up)*, **sírvelas** *(serve them)*, **pica** *(cut)*, **remuévelo** *(stir it)*, **pon** *(add)*, and **mezcla** *(mix)*. Then, read the list of verbs to the class and demonstrate them. Have students guess the meaning of what you are saying.

3. **Writing:** Have students write the infinitives of the verbs mentioned in Activity 2. Explain to students that in many cases, verbs in recipes appear in infinitive form rather than command form.

4. **Pair work/Writing:** Have pairs of students write a conversation for the following situation: they are preparing for a party, but they need help. Have them use the functions and vocabulary from this **paso** to delegate the remaining preparatory tasks—including preparation of the tacos—to two or three friends.

5. **Speaking:** Have partners act out and present to the class the conversation they wrote for Activity 4.

6. **Culture:** The word *chile* comes to Spanish and English from náhuatl, the language of the Aztecs. Chiles have been an important ingredient in the cuisines of Mexico for thousands of years. Ask students if they have ever tasted **jalapeño** chiles, or if they know where they come from. On a map of Mexico, point out the state of Jalapa and explain that the adjective **jalapeño/a** means *from Jalapa*, and that some dishes from this region are characterized by the use of this type of chile. Other chiles students may be familiar with are **serranos** and **poblanos**.

Realia 10-3: Electronic mail

1. **Reading:** Have students read the e-mail and list the preterite verbs they can identify. Also, have them make a list of the unfamiliar words and cognates in the letter and work in pairs to try to figure out their meaning.

2. **Listening:** Read aloud the letter and ask the students true or false questions to test their comprehension.

3. **Writing:** Have students write a narrative about what they did last New Year's Eve. You may want to review the preterite with them.

4. **Pair work/Writing:** In pairs, have students reread the electronic letter and write a response to Dolores.

5. **Culture:** During the 12 days leading up to Christmas, Mexicans reenact the Holy Family's search for an inn. This celebration is called **Posada** or **Las posadas**. A group of people carry candles from house to house, knocking on doors and singing a song in which they request lodging for the Holy Family. The owners of the houses refuse again and again, until the participants finally arrive at a pre-chosen host's house. A party at this house includes **buñuelos** *(sweet fritters)*, **tamales** *(a cornmeal crust filled with meat and wrapped in corn husks)*, additional singing, and a **piñata**.

servicio de

DEPORTES

Actividad	Días	Horario
BADMINTON, JUEGOS ALTERNATIVOS	M y J, Ult. juev. de mes	13'55 - 15'55 13'55 - 15'45
GIMNASIA MANTENIMIENTO	M y J	13'55 - 14'50 1.º turno 14'50 - 15'45 2.º turno
DANZA	M y J	20'30 - 21'30
GIMNASIA MANTENIMIENTO	L, X y V	21'15 - 22'15
SAUNA (1 hora /persona)	L	20'00 - 21'00 21'00 - 22'00
SQUASH (1/2 hora/persona)	L, X y V	17'00 - 18'00
PISCINA (sólo usuarios otras actividades)	L, M, X, J y V	22'00 - 22'30
RUGBY	M y J	21'30 - 22'45
NATACIÓN	L, M, X, J y V	15'00 - 16'00 1.º turno 16'00 - 17'00 2.º turno
ATLETISMO	L, M, X, J y V	19'00 -21'00 1.º turno / 2.º turno
TENIS DE MESA	M y J	14'00 - 15'00 1.º turno / 2.º turno
JUDO	L, X y V	14'00 - 15'00 1.º turno / 2.º turno
DANZA	M y J	14'00 - 15'00 1.º turno / 2.º turno

La Universidad de Cádiz quiere ofrecerte la posibilidad de participar en actividades culturales y deportivas, para contribuir a tu desarrollo personal a través de una mejor utilización del ocio.

El Vicerrectorado de Extensión Universitaria, a través de su Servicio de Deportes, pone a tu disposición una serie de actividades recreativas y de competición, que te van a proporcionar la oportunidad de conocer nuevos deportes en un ambiente agradable y divertido, donde lo importante es la participación y la relación con los demás, y no el nivel de habilidad.

Course schedule for physical education classes from "Actividades de promoción" and "Introducción" from brochure, *Universidad de Cádiz, Extensión Universitaria, Servicio de Deportes.* Reprinted by permission of **Universidad de Cádiz, Servicio de Deportes.**

Realia 11-2

Por qué me gusta el windsurf

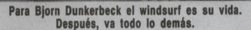

Para Bjorn Dunkerbeck el windsurf es su vida. Después, va todo lo demás.

"No hay límites en el windsurf y eso es bueno".

"Es un deporte que recomendaría a mucha gente, sobre todo a los que tienen estrés. Relaja un montón".

Y, un consejo: "Para aprender es importante ir a una escuela. Se aprende mucho más rápido que si lo haces por tu cuenta.

"No me gustan los deportes como el golf o el tenis en los que no existe riesgo. Me gustan los deportes que se practican en solitario, en los que tú eres el único responsable de que todo salga bien".

Carné de identidad
Nacido en: la localidad de Ribe (Dinamarca), el 16 de julio de 1969.
Mide: 1,91 metros.
Pesa: 90 kilos.
Odia: los días sin viento.
Deportes: windsurf, windsurf y windsurf. Si no puede salir al mar, se conforma con la bici de montaña.

From "Primera clase Bjorn y Britt Dunkerbeck" from *Gente Ce,* year V, no. 6 August/1994. Copyright " 1994 by *EN & B Revistas, Hispano Francesa de Ediciones (Spain)* Reprinted by permission of publisher.

Querido Miguel:

   ¿Cómo estás? Yo estoy bien alegre porque las vacaciones de verano empiezan dentro de poco. ¿Qué tal el equipo de fútbol? ¿Ganaron ustedes el partido contra las panteras de Filadelfia? Espero que sí. El sábado pasado nuestro equipo perdió el partido contra los vaqueros de Bayamón. Es que tuvimos mala suerte porque nuestro jugador estrella estaba enfermo. ¡Qué mala suerte!

   No tengo mucho que contarte pues no hice muchas cosas la semana pasada. El lunes jugué al tenis con mi hermana Marisol. Claro que ella me ganó. Mi hermana es una gran tenista. Estoy orgulloso de ella. Antes de que se me olvide, ¿cuándo vienes a visitarnos? Mis padres te aprecian mucho y a mí me gusta mucho compartir contigo. Tú eres mi mejor amigo. ¿Te acuerdas cuando fuimos al parque de atracciones con Ada y Edna? Compramos boletos para todas las atracciones: la montaña rusa, los carritos locos, el paracaídas, el bote pirata, etc. ¡Qué divertido!

   Bueno, tengo que estudiar para un examen mañana. Dime, ¿te gusta vivir en Nueva York? Escribe pronto y cuéntame cómo son tus nuevos amigos de la escuela. Saludos a tu familia.

Tu amigo,

David

David A. Cancel García
URB. Parque Real
Calle Rey núm 822
Bayamón, P.R. 00956

REALIA

Realia 11-1: Sports brochure from Universidad de Cádiz

1. **Reading/Speaking:** Have students read the two paragraphs in the lefthand column and ask for an oral summary.

2. **Reading:** Ask students to suggest a health and fitness schedule at the University of Cádiz for the following people:
   - an older student who is returning to college after raising a family
   - a busy single parent who would like to work out every day
   - an 18-year-old student who enjoys contact sports
   - a 20-year-old female student who is in a wheelchair
   - themselves
   Students should be able to explain their choices.

3. **Pair work/Speaking:** Divide the class into pairs. Have pairs role-play the parts of two students. One student in each pair is very fit and healthy and involved in sports, the other is out of shape, but wants to be more physically active. The fit student should inquire about the second student's interests and suggest classes and other health-related activities to help that person achieve his or her fitness goals.

4. **Culture:** Have students look over the **Días** column on the schedule. Ask them to find the days when **natación**, **squash**, **atletismo**, and **judo** are offered. What do students think the capital letters L, M, X, J and V stand for? Can they figure out what X means in this context? Explain that in Spain it is common to abbreviate days of the week with capital letters, and to avoid confusion with **martes**, **miércoles** is often abbreviated as **X** or **Mi**. Then have students look at the **Horario** column, and find the times when one can use the sauna or pool, or play rugby. Does it seem unusual to students that these facilities are available at 9:00 and 10:00 in the evening? Remind students that in Spain, especially in the south, people tend to be active later in the evening than in the U.S.

Realia 11-2: Windsurf article

1. **Reading:** Have students read over the article. Ask them to pay special attention to cognates and context. Make a list of unfamiliar words and phrases they find difficult and help them guess their meaning: **riesgo, en solitario, montón, por tu cuenta.** Ask them to read the **Carné de identidad** and to describe Bjorn. What is Bjorn's advice? What does he do for relaxation?

2. **Listening:** Select students at random to read aloud the article in sections. Ask the class questions about each section. How does his discipline and training help keep Bjorn master of the waves **(el amo de las olas)**? Ask the class what other sports are both fun and good for them.

3. **Speaking:** Divide the class into small groups. Have them use vocabulary from the **Segundo paso** to ask each other questions about moods, physical conditions, and to give each other advice.

4. **Writing:** Ask students to write a paragraph using this lesson's vocabulary. Have them recommend sports that develop the muscles in a certain part of the body and can help when a person is also nervous or worried. What do they recommend in regard to care and participation in the sports if a person is ill? (**tener fiebre, dolerle la espalda, etc.**)

5. **Culture:** You might point out to students that North American sports, such as rollerblading (**patinar en línea**) and windsurfing (**la tabla de vela**), are very popular in many Spanish-speaking countries. Ask students to make a list of other North American sports that people in Latin American countries participate in.

Realia 11-3: Personal letter

1. **Reading/Listening:** Have students work in pairs to read the letter and create a brief outline of the main points contained in it: **las vacaciones de verano, el equipo de fútbol, el tenis,** and so on. Ask students true/false questions to test their comprehension.

2. **Speaking:** Have students write a telephone conversation between David and Miguel in which Miguel calls David after getting his friend's letter. You may want to have them perform and record their conversations for their Portfolios.

3. **Pair work/Speaking:** Have students work in pairs to ask each other questions about their activities of the past week. They can base some of their questions on the letter.

4. **Writing:** Ask students to write a reply to the letter and tell about their activities for the past week.

5. **Culture:** In some Spanish-speaking cities, people don't have mail delivery to their homes. In many cases, people have a mail box at a central post office where they go to pick up their mail. The address on the these letters identifies an **apartado** or **casilla** *(post office box)* with a number instead of a street address. In other towns and cities people have a **buzón** *(mail box)* outside the house close to the street and the postman delivers the mail every two or three days. Everybody gets to know **el cartero** because he tycally keeps the same route until retirement.

Realia 12-1

Mallorca

¡Una isla fascinante!

¿Que te gustaría hacer este verano? ¿Estás aburrido? No te quedes en casa. Palma de Mallorca te ofrece las vacaciones ideales. La isla es famosa por sus bellezas naturales, sus playas, y su excelente clima. Es el lugar favorito del turismo nacional e internacional. Ven a pasar tus vacaciones a Mallorca. Lo único que necesitas llevar es tu maleta, tu cámara , tus lentes de sol y tu bronceador para poder divertirte. La comida es muy rica, en especial los mariscos. Las playas son maravillosas y puedes bucear, practicar el kayak de mar, el veleo, nadar o simplemente visitar sus playas para asolearte. El calor y la amabilidad de la gente te esperan en Palma de Mallorca.

REALIA

¿A USTEDES LES GUSTA IR AL CAMPO?

Radio Castellano entrevistó a varios estudiantes de Escuela Superior en diferentes lugares donde se habla español. Las siguientes fueron sus opiniones sobre el campo.

"El campo para pasar mis vacaciones"

"Me gusta mucho el campo porque puedo descansar y pescar... Además en la casa de campo de mi familia tenemos tres perros, dos caballos y muchas ovejas. Mi tío Rafael cuida nuestro rancho. Es un lugar maravilloso pero sólo por una temporada; me hacen falta la ciudad, mis amigos, la escuela, la biblioteca, los cines, ..."

San Antonio, Texas: Camille, 16 años

"Me encanta la ciudad"

"No me gusta para nada el campo: tanto silencio, tanta soledad, tantos animales... La ciudad es lo mío: muchísimo ruido, gente caminando y hablando, coches y tiendas por todas partes... ¡A mí me fascina la ciudad! ¡No hay nada como vivir en una metrópoli!"

Ciudad Juárez, México: Edith, 17 años

"El campo es fantástico"

"Yo vivo en un pueblo, aunque voy al colegio en la capital. Me gusta mucho vivir aquí; no paso el calor del verano pero tenemos una piscina. Me gusta mucho compartir con la gente y jugar al soccer. Es más saludable vivir lejos de la contaminación..."

Granada, España: Javier, 14 años, Alumno de 1° de ESO

Realia 12-3

GUATEMALA:
"Fuiste a Guatemala. La comida y los hoteles son muy baratos. Recibe $80."

COLOMBIA:
"Te encantan los platos típicos de este país, por eso sales a comer demasiado. Da $30."

BOLIVIA:
"En Bolivia compraste regalos muy bonitos para toda tu familia. Da $30."

URUGUAY:
"Aquí quieres tomar el sol y descansar en la playa, pero no llevaste tu traje de baño. Da $20."

PERÚ:
"¡Tus papás te regalaron un viaje al Perú! Allí vas a escalar montañas. Recibe $100."

Cárcel
Paga $40.

Panamá

Costa Rica

Nicaragua

Honduras

El Salvador

Guatemala

Aeropuerto
Paga $10.

Colombia

América Central

República Dominicana

Aduana
Paga $30.

Países Andinos

Turisteando

Norteamérica y El Caribe

Aduana
Paga $20.

Ecuador

Puerto Rico

Bolivia

Cuba

Perú

México

Chile

¡No llevaste tu pasaporte! Ve a la cárcel.

Sudamérica y España

Estación de Tren
Paga $20.

Paraguay

Venezuela

Aduana
Paga $20.

Uruguay

Argentina

España

Salida
Recibe $100.

PARAGUAY:
"Fuiste a Paraguay, pero todo es muy caro. Da $80."

COSTA RICA:
"Ganaste un viaje a Costa Rica. Vas a hacer turismo y explorar la selva. Recibe $100."

REPÚBLICA DOMINICANA:
"Fuiste a República Dominicana con lentes de sol y bloqueador pero hizo mal tiempo. Ve al aeropuerto y da $10."

CHILE:
"Fuiste a las montañas en Chile pero no llevaste los esquís. Ve a la estación de tren y da $5."

EL SALVADOR:
"Te quedas en la casa de tus amigos salvadoreños. Recibe $75."

REALIA

Realia 12-1: Tourist brochure

1. **Reading:** Have students read the brochure. Ask them to identify the natural attractions and activities the tourist ads from Mallorca offer to the tourist.

2. **Speaking:** Ask students to imagine they are staying on the island, and to tell the class activities they plan on doing during their stay. Have students use different verb + infinitive expressions and the information in the hotel ad. (**Esta tarde, quiero jugar al tenis. Por la noche, voy a cenar en un restaurante en la playa. Mañana, pienso nadar y hacer ejercicio.**)

3. **Group work/Speaking/Writing:** Divide the class into small groups. Students in each group are planning to take a vacation together. They must agree on the following: where to go, how long they will stay, where to stay (**hotel, parador**), and what to see. When students reach an agreement, have them prepare their travel itinerary. You may want to ask students to present their group's travel plans to the class.

4. **Culture:** Have students locate the Balearic Islands on a map. Throughout history, the Balearic Islands have been occupied by different peoples: among them the Iberians, Phoenicians, Greeks, Carthaginians, Romans, and Byzantines. A regiment of Balearic islanders became famous as stone slingers in Julius Caesar's armies. During the late 700's the Moors invaded the islands, and in 1235 Aragon took back all the islands except for Minorca. A mild climate and the islanders' relaxed way of life have made the islands a major tourist destination for visitors worldwide. Majorca, the largest island, has good harbors, and grapes, olives, oranges, and other fruits flourish there. Manufactured goods such as shoes, ceramics, and metalware are very important industries, especially in Majorca.

Realia 12-2: Interviews

1. **Reading/Speaking:** Explain to students that this reading contains responses from teenagers about which is better: being in the city or the country while on vacation. Give students 2–3 minutes to read over the responses and find the answers to the following questions:
   • Who prefers the city?
   • Who prefers the country?
   • What person lists good and bad things about each?
   After students have a general idea of the content, you may ask them to read for more detail and find the following information:
   • What do Javier and Camille like about being in the country?
   • What are some of the drawbacks Camille lists about being in the country?
   • What are two advantages to being in the city, according to Camille and Edith?

2. **Writing/Pair work:** Have students imagine that they are going to take a trip to any of the places they have learned about this year in Spanish class. Allow them 2–3 minutes to make some notes about why they would like to visit that place, what they would like to do and see there, and so forth. Ask students to work with a partner and alternate playing the role of a travel agent and tourist. The agent should ask about the person's plans, and the tourist should try to get more information about his or her travel destination from the agent. Students may use their notes during the conversations.

Activities for Communication **133**

3. **Group work:** Divide the class into groups of four. Each group will role-play the following characters: a real estate agent, a secretary, and two clients. Have each group interview the clients to obtain information about their interests, including what each one likes to do. Match each client with the area **(campo** or **ciudad)** that best meets his or her needs. Ask them to report to the class.

4. **Culture:** Have students look at the way the last response is signed, and ask them what they think **Alumnos del 1° de ESO** means. It stands for **Educación Secundaria Obligatoria**, and is the course of study following grade school in Spain. These students are in their first year of this course, and are 13 to 14 years old.

Realia 12-3: Board game

1. **Reading:** Have students look over the game board and read the messages on the instruction cards. Can they figure out more or less how this game is meant to be played?

2. **Listening:** Make statements about various activities that you can do in different Spanish-speaking countries. Students tell you which "country" you are in, based on the information given in the game. Vary this by saying which "country" you're in and have students tell you what activities you will be able to do there, according to the game.

3. **Reading/Group work:** Have students work in small groups to play the game. Students should take turns reading the captions on the cards aloud for each other.

4. **Writing:** Have students write out a brief itinerary of the "countries" they went to while playing the game. What did they do in each place they visited? Where else did they go? (Note: To prepare for this, have students jot down their itinerary while playing the game.)

5. **Speaking:** Ask students which cards they would like to get, and why. Which Spanish-speaking country would they most like to visit?

6. **Culture:** In some Latin American countries currency is named after European explorers and heroes of the Latin American independence movement: **colón** (for Christopher Columbus) in Costa Rica; **balboa** (for Vasco Núñez de Balboa) in Panamá; **bolívar** (for Simón Bolívar) in Venezuela; and **sucre** (for Antonio José de Sucre) in Ecuador. Ask students to do research in the library on the background of these famous people. You may also ask which U.S. presidents are on the different denominations of the dollar.

REALIA

Situation Cards

Situation Cards 1-1, 1-2, 1-3: Interview

Situation 1-1: Interview

I am a new student at your school. I want to make new friends, so I talk to you, trying to break the ice. How do you respond to my questions?

Buenas tardes.
¿Cómo estás?
Soy... ¿Cómo te llamas tú?
(Introduce me to someone else in the class.)
Bueno, tengo que irme. Hasta luego.

Situation 1-2: Interview

I want to get to know you and your friends a little better, so I'm asking you some questions. How do you respond?

Yo tengo ... años. ¿Y tú? ¿Cuántos años tienes?
Yo soy de... ¿De dónde eres?
¿Cómo se llama tu amigo(a)?
¿Cuántos años tiene...?
¿De dónde es...?

Situation 1-3: Interview

I want to find out what you like and don't like. How do you respond to these questions?

¿Qué te gusta?
¿Te gusta la comida italiana?
¿Qué no te gusta?
¿Te gusta el baloncesto?
¿Te gusta la clase de inglés?

¡Ven conmigo! Level 1, Chapter 1   Activities for Comm

138

Situation Cards 1-1, 1-2, 1-3: Role-playing

Situation 1-1: Role-playing

Student A   You're at a party one evening and you see **Student B**, someone you would like to meet. You greet **Student B** and ask how he or she is doing. Then ask what his or her name is. Respond to the questions that **Student B** asks you. Then respond appropriately to the last thing that **Student B** says to you.

Student B   You're at a party one evening and **Student A** starts to talk to you. Answer his or her questions, then find out **Student A's** name. When **Student A** answers, say that you're pleased to meet him or her.

Situation 1-2: Role-playing

Student A   **Student B** sits down next to you in the school cafeteria. You haven't met yet, but you know that **Student B** is in your English class. Greet **Student B** and tell him or her your name. Ask **Student B** his or her name and find out how old he or she is.

Student B   You're a new student at school. In the cafeteria you sit next to **Student A**, a student from your English class whom you haven't met yet. Answer **Student A's** questions and then find out how old he or she is.

Situation 1-3: Role-playing

Student A   You and **Student B** want to go out to eat. Find out if he or she likes the following kinds of food: Italian, Chinese, Mexican. After hearing **Student B's** responses, tell him or her that you also like pizza.

Student B   You and **Student A** want to go out to eat. Your friend asks you several questions about what kind of food you like. Answer the questions and then tell **Student A** that you like pizza very much. Ask **Student A** if he or she likes pizza too.

SITUATION CARDS

Situation Cards 2-1, 2-2, 2-3: Interview

Situation 2-1: Interview

You and I are going to go shopping for school supplies together. I want to know what things you need and what you already have. How would you answer my questions?

¿Tienes bolígrafos y papel para la clase de inglés?

¿Cuántos cuadernos necesitas para el colegio?

¿Qué necesitas para la clase de español?

¿Quieres una mochila nueva?

Situation 2-2: Interview

I want to know what your room at home is like, and I want you to tell me a little about your school. You can create an imaginary room or school if you wish. Respond to my questions.

¿Qué hay en tu cuarto?

¿Cuántos carteles hay en la clase de español?

¿Tienes mucha tarea en la clase de inglés?

Situation 2-3: Interview

I want to know what you want and need to do today.

¿Qué quieres hacer?

¿Qué necesitas hacer primero?

¿Necesitas organizar tu cuarto?

SITUATION CARDS

Situation 2-1: Role-playing

Student A   Imagine it is the first day of school and you and **Student B** are discussing what school supplies you have and don't have. Greet **Student B** and then ask her or him what supplies she or he has for school. Then answer the question **Student B** asks you.

Student B   Imagine it is the first day of school and you and **Student A** are discussing what school supplies you have and don't have. After greeting **Student A**, answer her or his question with at least four items. Then ask **Student A** what school supplies she or he doesn't have.

Situation 2-2: Role-playing

Student A   You and **Student B** are comparing your rooms. By asking questions, find out if **Student B** has a TV, a table, some posters, a clock, or a desk in his or her room.

Student B   You and **Student A** are comparing your rooms. First, answer his or her questions, then ask **Student A** if he or she has a lamp, a radio, or some magazines in the room.

Situation 2-3: Role-playing

Student A   You are discussing what you want to do after school with **Student B**. Tell him or her what you need to do first, then at least two things you want to do. Then ask **Student B** what he or she needs and wants to do after school today.

Student B   You and **Student A** are discussing what you need and want to do after school. Listen to **Student A's** plans and then answer her or his question with at least two things you need to do and two things that you want to do.

¡Ven conmigo! Level 1, Chapter 2

Situation 3-1: Interview

It's the morning of the first day of school and I'm talking to you in the hallway just as the bell is about to ring. I want to find out what this semester will be like for you. Respond to my questions.

¿Qué clases tienes este semestre?

Y hoy, ¿qué clase tienes primero?

Y después, ¿qué clases tienes?

¿Qué hora es?

Situation 3-2: Interview

As we are walking from one class to another, I ask you questions about your schedule for this semester. Answer my questions.

¿A qué hora tienes...?

¿Qué clase tienes a la una?

¿A qué hora tienes el almuerzo?

¿Tienes prisa?

Situation 3-3: Interview

It's now the end of the first week of classes. I'm trying to get to know you better, so I ask you questions about yourself and about your impressions of the school: classes, teachers, classmates.

¿Cómo es la clase de ...?

¿Cómo son los profesores este semestre?

¿Cuál es tu clase favorita? ¿Por qué?

¿Te gustan los deportes/las fiestas/los conciertos/las novelas?

SITUATION CARDS

Situation Cards 3-1, 3-2, 3-3: Role-playing

Situation 3-1: Role-playing

Student A   You and **Student B** meet and compare your school schedules. Greet each other. Then answer his or her question. Ask what classes he or she has this semester. Listen to your friend's reply and then answer his or her question about the time.

Student B   You run into **Student A** and compare school schedules. After answering your friend's greeting, ask him or her what classes he or she has this semester. Tell your friend what classes you have this semester, then ask him or her what time it is. After he or she tells you, say that you have to go.

Situation 3-2: Role-playing

Student A   You and **Student B** are trying to complete a school schedule together. Your friend knows what the classes are, and you know when the classes meet. Answer your partner's questions, using the following times:
1. 10:00 A.M.   2. 1:30 P.M.   3. 8:45 A.M.   4. 3:10 P.M.

Student B   You and **Student A** are trying to complete a school schedule. You know what the classes are and your partner knows at what time the classes meet. Ask your partner at what time are the following classes:
1. Spanish   2. Math   3. Computer Science   4. Art

Situation 3-3: Role-playing

Student A   You and **Student B** are discussing your teachers. Begin the conversation by asking your partner what your Spanish teacher is like. Then answer your partner's question with at least three descriptive adjectives.

Student B   You and **Student A** are discussing your teachers. Tell your partner at least three qualities that your Spanish teacher has. Then ask your partner what his or her English teacher is like.

¡Ven conmigo! Level 1, Chapter 3

Situation Cards 4-1, 4-2, 4-3: Interviews

Situation 4-1: Interview

I am an exhange student interested in finding out what a typical teenager from the United States does outside of class. How would you answer these questions?

¿Qué te gusta hacer con tus amigos?
¿Te gusta mirar la televisión en tu tiempo libre?
¿Tocas el piano?
¿Qué deportes practicas?

Situation 4-2: Interview

I need your help in locating some things. Tell me where they are.

¿Hay una piscina cerca de tu casa?
¿Tu casa está lejos o cerca de la escuela?
¿Qué hay encima de tu escritorio?
¿Dónde está tu libro de español?
¿Quién está al lado de...? (*name a student in the class*)

Situation 4-3: Interview

Tell me where and when you do the following activities at the mentioned times.

¿Cuándo vas al cine?
¿Cuándo practicas los deportes?
¿Dónde estás los lunes a las diez de la mañana?
¿Qué haces los sábados?

SITUATION CARDS

Situation Cards 4-1, 4-2, 4-3: Role-playing

Situation 4-1 : Role-playing

Student A   You and **Student B** are discussing what each of you does in your free time. Ask **Student B** what he or she does.

Student B   You respond to **Student A** and say what you do in your free time. Then ask **Student A** what he or she does.

        ¿Que haces...?   descanso   hablo por teléfono
        ¿Qué te gusta hacer?   camino con el perro
                                     trabajo

Situation 4-2: Role-playing

Student A   You are new in town and want to find out where some places are located. Ask **Student B** if the following places are far from or close to the school: the movie theater, the swimming pool, the post office.

Student B   Listen to **Student A**'s questions and tell him or her if the places are far from or close to the school.

        cerca de   lejos de

Situation 4-3: Role-playing

Student A   You and **Student B** are discussing plans for the week-end. Ask **Student B** where he or she is going Saturday.

Student B   Answer **Student A**'s questions and then ask where he or she is going on Sunday.

        ¿Adónde vas?

SITUATION CARDS

Situation 5-1: Interview

I am conducting a survey in order to know more about you and your classmates. I would like to know what things you do and how frequently you do them. Help me by answering the following questions.

¿Quiénes en la clase tocan la guitarra?

¿Quién cuida a su hermano/a durante la semana?

¿Ayudas en casa todos los días?

¿Con qué frecuencia hablas por teléfono?

Situation 5-2: Interview

I am a foreign visitor and I am curious about what you and your friends like to do together. How would you answer these questions?

¿Qué les gusta hacer durante el fin de semana?

¿Les gusta hacer ejercicio juntos?

¿Escriben cartas o miran la televisión los sábados por la noche?

¿Siempre leen las tiras cómicas los domingos?

Situation 5-3: Interview

My family is thinking about moving to your city. Can you give me some information about the weather?

¿Qué tiempo hace en la primavera?

¿Nieva mucho en el invierno?

¿Hace buen tiempo en el verano?

¿En qué meses hace calor?

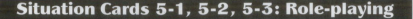

Situation 5-1: Role-playing

Student A You and **Student B** want to compare how often you do certain activities. Choose three of the following activities and ask **Student B** how often he or she does them: ride a bike, study in the library, organize your room, spend time with friends, take the bus to school.

Student B You and **Student A** want to compare how often you do certain activities. Answer **Student A**'s questions and then find out how often he or she does three of the activities.

¿**Con qué frecuencia?** nunca   siempre   a veces

Situation 5-2: Role-playing

Student A Interview **Student B** and find out which of the following he or she likes to do: to read newspapers or magazines, to exercise or to scuba dive, to read the comics or to write postcards. Then answer **Student B**'s questions.

Student B Answer **Student A**'s questions, telling which you prefer. Then ask which of the following **Student B** likes: to fish or to ski, to run along the beach or to run in the park, to study or to attend an aerobic exercise class.

¿**Te gusta más...?**   pescar   bucear   leer revistas
leer las tiras cómicas

Situation 5-3: Role-playing

Student A Pretend you are traveling to the United States for the very first time. You want to know what the weather is like in several cities during the spring and summer so you can decide which ones to visit. Ask **Student B** about the weather in the following places: Miami, Alaska, Chicago, San Antonio.

Student B **Student A** is traveling to the United States for the first time. Answer his or her questions about the weather in the spring and summer. Then switch roles.

¿**Qué tiempo hace...?**   **Llueve.**   **Nieva.**
Hace fresco.   **Hace mucho viento.**   **Hace calor.**

Situation Cards 6-1, 6-2, 6-3: Interview

Situation 6-1: Interview

Tell me about your family or an imaginary one.

¿Cuántas personas hay en tu familia?

¿Quiénes son?

¿Tienen Uds. un perro o un gato?

¿Quién en tu familia es cómico?

Situation 6-2: Interview

Think of a person you know well and really like and answer my questions about that person.

¿Cómo se llama tu amigo/a?

¿Cuántos años tiene?

¿De qué color son los ojos?

¿Cómo es? Por ejemplo, ¿es travieso o cómico?

Situation 6-3: Interview

I need your advice. Tell me what I should do in each situation.

Tengo un examen mañana en la clase de biología, pero quiero salir con mis amigos. ¿Qué debo hacer?

Mis abuelos van a visitar esta noche, pero la casa es un desastre. ¿Qué debemos hacer?

Quiero ir al centro comercial con mi amigo, pero tengo mucha tarea. ¿Qué debo hacer?

SITUATION CARDS

Situation Cards 6-1, 6-2, 6-3: Role-playing

Situation 6-1: Role-playing

Student A You and **Student B** are talking about your families, real or imaginary. Ask **Student B** if he or she has a large or small family. Also find out how many brothers and/or sisters **Student B** has. Ask if he or she has a cat or dog. Then answer **Student B**'s questions.

Student B You and **Student A** are talking about your real or imaginary families. Answer **Student A**'s questions about your family and then ask him or her how many people are in his or her family. Also ask how old his or her brothers and/or sisters are.

¿Tienes...?   ¿Cuántos/as?

Situation 6-2: Role-playing

Student A Imagine you are talking long distance to **Student B** who is an exchange student coming to live with you soon. Introduce yourself and give **Student B** a detailed description of yourself and your personality. Then ask **Student B** what he or she is like.

Student B Imagine you are an exchange student talking long distance to **Student A** who soon will be your host in the U.S. Listen to his or her description and then answer **Student A**'s question.

Tengo...   los ojos   travieso/a   cariñoso/a

Situation 6-3: Role-playing

Student A You and **Student B** are comparing the things you have to do around the house to help out. Tell **Student B** two chores that you do and then ask **Student B** what he or she does.

Student B You and **Student A** are comparing chores you do around the house. Listen to what **Student A** does and then answer his or her question, telling two or three things you do to help out.

lavar   limpiar   pasar la aspiradora

HRW material copyrighted under notice appearing earlier in this work.

SITUATION CARDS

Situation Cards 7-1, 7-2, 7-3: Interview

Situation 7-1: Interview

I call you on the telephone to talk to your brother, but he's not home. How do you answer my questions?

Aló. ¿Está tu hermano?

¿Dónde está?

¿A qué hora regresa?

¿Puedo dejar un recado?

Situation 7-2: Interview

I have called to see if you are planning to come to my party. How do you respond to my questions?

¿Piensas venir a mi fiesta esta noche?

¿A qué hora vienes, a las ocho o a las nueve?

¿Estás listo/a?

¿Qué necesitas hacer antes de la fiesta?

Situation 7-3: Interview

I invite you to do several activities but you have other plans. Turn down my invitations in as many different ways as you can and explain why.

¿Te gustaría ir al parque conmigo hoy?

¿Quieres venir a mi casa esta noche?

Tengo ganas de nadar. ¿Quieres ir a la piscina ahora?

¿Prefieres ir a la piscina mañana?

Pues, ¿te gustaría ir a nadar el domingo?

SITUATION CARDS

Situation 7-1: Role-playing

Student A   When you call your best friend, **Student B** answers. Say hello and ask for your friend. Respond appropriately to the information you get from **Student B**. If your friend isn't home, tell **Student B** you will call back later and say goodbye.

Student B   **Student A** calls asking for a friend. Answer the phone and tell **Student A** that you are sorry his or her friend is not home. Find out who is calling. Answer any questions **Student A** asks and respond when **Student A** says goodbye.

Situation 7-2: Role-playing

Student A   You and **Student B** are about to leave for the movies. You don't want to be late but **Student B** seems to be having trouble getting ready. Ask if **Student B** is ready now and then ask what he or she needs to do. Repeat the questions until **Student B** is ready.

Student B   **Student A** has arrived at your house and is anxious to leave for the movies. You are trying to stall because you and your friends have planned a surprise party for **Student A**. When **Student A** asks, keep telling him or her you aren't ready. After the third time, say you're ready.

Situation 7-3: Role-playing

Student A   **Student B** is famous for making excuses not to do things. Call him or her up and extend invitations to several events or activities on the weekend. **Student B** will decline and give an excuse for not doing the activity with you.

Student B   Your friend **Student A** really wants you to do something with him or her this weekend, but you have no desire or intention to do anything. You just want to stay at home and relax. Decline all invitations that **Student A** gives you and give reasons for declining.

Situation 8-1: Interview

Imagine I'm an exchange student new to the United States. Answer my questions about food and meals.

¿Qué comes para el desayuno?

¿Quién prepara el desayuno en tu familia?

¿A qué hora almuerzas?

¿En qué consiste un almuerzo típico en los Estados Unidos?

Situation 8-2: Interview

Imagine you work at a cafeteria and I come through the line with the following questions about the food. How would you respond?

¿Están muy picantes los frijoles?

¿Cómo está el postre hoy?

¿Qué frutas hay hoy?

¿Qué sándwiches hay?

Situation 8-3: Interview

Imagine I'm a customer in a restaurant and you're the server. How would you respond?

Camarero/a, ¿me puede traer el menú, por favor?

Camarero/a, este tenedor está sucio.

¿Me puede traer la cuenta?

¿Está incluida la propina?

SITUATION CARDS

Situation Cards 8-1, 8-2, 8-3: Role-playing

Situation 8-1: Role-playing

Student A Imagine you like a light breakfast and **Student B** likes a heavy one. Tell **Student B** your opinion and include what you typically eat. Then ask **Student B** what he or she eats for breakfast.

Student B **Student A** doesn't eat much and you like to eat a lot for breakfast! Listen to what **Student A** says about his or her typical breakfast. Then answer **Student A**'s question. Include at least five different items that you enjoy eating for breakfast.

ligero   fuerte   el cereal   los huevos   típicamente

Situation 8-2: Role-playing

Student A Imagine that you and **Student B** are eating dinner at a restaurant. **Student B** asks you several questions about how your food tastes. Let **Student B** know if the foods taste salty, cold, hot, or delicious.

Student B Imagine that you and **Student A** are eating dinner at a restaurant. Ask **Student A** how the following items taste: the soup, the chicken, the vegetables, and the dessert.

¿Cómo está(n)?   salado   rico   caliente   frío
el pollo   el postre   la sopa   las legumbres

Situation 8-3: Role-playing

Student A Imagine that you're a server and **Student B** is your customer. Ask **Student B** if he or she wants dessert. Then bring **Student B** the bill. Tell him or her how much it is and that the tip isn't included.

Student B You have just finished your meal at a restaurant and **Student B** is your server. Answer **Student A**'s question and tell him or her what you want for dessert. After ordering dessert, ask **Student A** for the bill. Then ask **Student A** if the tip is included.

postre   ¿Está incluida la propina?   Voy a pedir...

Situation Cards 9-1, 9-2, 9-3: Interview

Situation 9-1: Interview

Imagine you need to buy gifts for your friends and family. How would you respond to these questions about shopping?

A tu amiga le gusta mucho la música. ¿Qué piensas comprarle para su cumpleaños?

¿Prefieres comprarle una corbata o una cartera a tu papá?

¿Qué piensas comprar en la juguetería?

¿Para quién son los aretes?

Situation 9-2: Interview

We are discussing what clothing you wear for certain occasions. How would you respond?

Por lo general, ¿qué ropa llevas cuando vas a la escuela?

¿Cuándo llevas ropa más formal?

Cuando hace mucho calor, ¿qué te gusta llevar?

¿Qué llevas hoy?

Situation 9-3: Interview

We are discussing clothing preferences. How would you respond to the following questions?

¿Te gustan más las camisas de cuadros o las de rayas?

¿Cuál es más barato, un vestido de seda o uno de algodón?

¿Son tan caras las botas como las sandalias?

¿Estos zapatos que llevo hoy son feos o bonitos?

SITUATION CARDS

Situation Cards 9-1, 9-2, 9-3: Role-playing

Situation 9-1: Role-playing

Student A   You and **Student B** have been invited to a birthday party for your friend, Eva. Ask **Student B** if he or she is going to the party and what he or she is planning to give Eva. Then answer **Student B**'s question.

Student B   You and **Student A** have been invited to Eva's birthday party. Respond to **Student A**'s questions and then ask **Student A** what he or she is going to buy for Eva.

¿Vas...?   regalar   comprar   unos aretes un cartel

Situation 9-2: Role-playing

Student A   You and **Student B** are going to play a guessing game. Look around the room and choose one student, but don't tell **Student B** whom you have chosen. He or she will ask you questions about what the student is wearing. Answer until **Student B** guesses whom you have chosen. Then switch roles.

Student B   You and **Student A** are playing a guessing game. **Student A** has selected someone in the class and it's your job to find out who he or she is by asking questions about what the person is wearing. Then switch roles.

¿Lleva....?   un vestido rojo   una camiseta azul

Situation 9-3: Role-playing

Student A   You're a customer in a department store and **Student B** is the clerk. Ask how much several items cost and then say if the price is a bargain or too expensive. Choose four of the following items to ask about: this green shirt, that striped tie, this wool sweater, that yellow blouse, this leather jacket.

Student B   You're a clerk in a department store. **Student A** asks you how much several items cost. When telling the price repeat the name of each item to make sure you're both talking about the same item. Some of your prices are too high.

¿Cuánto cuesta...?   esta camisa verde

SITUATION CARDS

Situation 10-1: Interview

Imagine you're at a friend's house getting things ready for a party. Your friend's four-year-old brother is asking you a lot of questions. How would you answer him?

¿Qué estás haciendo?

¿Quién está colgando las decoraciones?

¿Por qué estás limpiando el patio?

¿Cómo celebras tu cumpleaños?

Situation 10-2: Interview

You're helping a friend prepare a surprise birthday party. Respond to the following requests. You should either agree to do the task or politely refuse.

¿Puedes ir al supermercado?

¿Me puedes traer los globos?

¿Me ayudas a cocinar?

¿Me haces el favor de limpiar la casa?

Situation 10-3: Interview

We haven't talked for some time and I am curious about what you've been doing. How would you respond to my questions?

¿Qué hiciste el verano pasado?

¿Qué hizo tu familia el domingo por la mañana?

¿Estudiaste español la semana pasada?

¿Trabajaste mucho o poco el año pasado?

SITUATION CARDS

Situation 10-1: Role-playing

Student A   You and **Student B** are talking about holidays. Ask **Student B** what his or her favorite holiday is and why it's his or her favorite one. Also ask how he or she celebrates that holiday. Then answer **Student B**'s questions.

Student B   You and **Student A** are talking about holidays. After answering **Student A**'s questions, ask **Student A** what his or her favorite holiday is and why. Also find out how he or she celebrates it.

día festivo   ¿Cómo?   el día de...

Situation 10-2: Role-playing

Student A   Imagine you're in charge of cleaning the house today. You want to finish quickly so you and **Student B** can go to the movies. Politely ask **Student B** to do at least three things to help you.

Student B   Imagine that you're helping **Student A** clean the house so the two of you can go to the movies. Respond to **Student A**'s requests and then add one more thing you can do to help.

¿Me ayudas a...?   ¿Me pasas...?   Haz   Pon
Claro que sí.   ¡Cómo no!   También puedo...

Situation 10-3: Role-playing

Student A   You and **Student B** are talking about what you did this weekend. Greet **Student B**, then ask if he or she had a good time. Then answer his or her questions including at least three different activities that you did and when you did them.

Student B   You and **Student A** are talking about what you did this weekend. Answer **Student A**'s questions. Include at least three things you did and when you did them. Then ask what he or she did.

el fin de semana   el viernes por la noche
el sábado   el domingo

SITUATION CARDS

Situation Cards 11-1, 11-2, 11-3: Interview

Situation 11-1: Interview

I'm curious about your lifestyle and daily routine. How would you respond to the following questions?

¿Qué tipo de ejercicio haces para llevar una vida sana?

¿Te estiras antes de hacer ejercicio?

¿Crees que en general llevas una vida sana?

Situation 11-2: Interview

Imagine you're in the doctor's office because you're not feeling well. Answer these questions the doctor asks you. Feel free to make up symptoms.

¿Cómo te sientes hoy?

¿Tienes fiebre?

¿Te parece que tienes gripe?

¿Qué más te duele?

Situation 11-3: Interview

Imagine it's Monday and you're telling me about your weekend. How would you respond to these questions?

¿Qué hiciste el sábado por la mañana?

¿Adónde fuiste el sábado por la noche?

¿Cuántas horas estudiaste el domingo?

¿Miraste un programa bueno en la tele este fin de semana?

SITUATION CARDS

Situation Cards 11-1, 11-2, 11-3: Role-playing

Situation 11-1: Role-playing

Student A Greet **Student B**, then ask how he or she is feeling. Invite **Student B** to go roller skating with you this afternoon. After hearing **Student B**'s answer tell him or her that maybe you can go another day.

Student B Respond to **Student A**'s greeting and then tell him or her that you're not feeling well. Decline **Student A**'s invitation, saying you're tired and really don't feel like roller skating today. Listen to **Student A**'s response and say you would like that very much.

patinar sobre ruedas

Situation 11-2: Role-playing

Student A You see **Student B** after school and notice that he or she doesn't look well. Greet **Student B** and then ask how he or she is feeling. After listening to what **Student B** tells you, respond appropriately.

Student B You're feeling sick when you run into **Student A** after school. Listen to **Student A**'s question and tell him or her that you think you have the flu. Also let **Student A** know what aches and just how you feel.

sentirse   doler   tener gripe

Situation 11-3: Role-playing

Student A You and **Student B** are comparing activities you did last week. Begin by asking **Student B** what he or she did on Monday. Take turns asking and answering about your activities to see who had the most exciting week.

Student B You and **Student A** are comparing activities you did last week. After answering **Student A**'s question, ask **Student A** what he or she did on Tuesday. Take turns asking and answering until you get to Sunday to see who had the more exciting week.

¿Qué hiciste?

SITUATION CARDS

Situation Cards 12-1, 12-2, 12-3: Interview

Situation 12-1: Interview

I would like to find out about what you do, like to do, and what you're planning to do this summer. How would you answer the following questions?

¿Qué haces después de clases?
¿Qué te gusta hacer los fines de semana?
¿Qué piensas hacer este verano?
¿Adónde quieres viajar?

Situation 12-2: Interview

I'm curious about where you would like go and what you would like to do on vacation. Imagine that you can go anywhere that you want to!

¿Adónde te gustaría ir este verano?
¿Qué tienes ganas de hacer?
¿Prefieres escalar montañas o saltar en paracaídas?

Situation 12-3: Interview

Tell me where you went and what you did on your last vacation. If you prefer, you can make up a vacation.

¿Adónde viajaste el verano pasado?
¿Adónde fueron tú y tu familia durante las vacaciones?
¿Qué hiciste cuando fuiste a _____?

SITUATION CARDS

Situation Cards 12-1, 12-2, 12-3: Role-playing

Situation 12-1: Role-playing

Student A — Greet **Student B**, then ask what he or she is planning to do this summer. Listen to **Student B**'s answer then respond to his or her questions about your summer plans by saying that you're planning to go to China this summer.

Student B — Respond to **Student A**'s greeting and then tell him or her that you are planning to go to Spain this summer. Then ask **Student A** what he or she plans to do this summer.

¿Qué piensas hacer...?   Pienso ir a...

Situation 12-2: Role-playing

Student A — Ask **Student B** where he or she would like to go this summer. Listen to his or her response then say that you have to stay home too. Next make plans with **Student B** to go camping.

Student B — Tell **Student A** that you would like to go to Puerto Rico this summer, but that you can't because you have to work. Then ask **Student A** where he or she would like to go this summer.

¿Adónde te gustaría ir?

Situation 12-3: Role-playing

Student A — Ask **Student B** where he or she went on vacation and what he or she did there. Listen to his or her response and then ask **Student B** if he or she has pictures of the trip.

Student B — Tell **Student A** that you went to Acapulco and went swimming, sailing, and had a great time. Then tell him or her that you don't have pictures because you didn't take along a camera.

¿Adónde fuiste de vacaciones?   Fui a...
ir de vela   ¿Tienes fotos?   No llevé...